THE High Chaparral

APACHE WAY

Authorized Edition

By STEVE FRAZEE

Cover by LARRY FREDERICK

WHITMAN BOOK DIVISION
WESTERN PUBLISHING COMPANY, INC., RACINE, WIS.

Contents

1   Quarrel   9

2   A Man to Ride With   20

3   "Amigo!"   28

4   The Enemy   39

5   A Glimpse of Sandy Lake   52

6   Apache Camp   63

7   A Saddle in Coral Wash   80

8   White Eyes   93

9   Vaquero and Buck   105

10   Strong of Heart   122

11   Flight   133

12   Cavalrymen   142

13   Ransom for the Captives   154

14   "A Terrible Mess"   168

15   Returning Friends   185

16   Brothers   196

1 Quarrel

THE GROUND was so hot that it burned through the soles of Billy Blue Cannon's boots as he crossed the yard of the High Chaparral ranch. His round face was gleaming with sweat and his shirt was soaked. The steady wind from the desert carried no coolness. It was keeping the windmill spinning, stirring the dust of the yard, and blistering everything it touched.

Blue came under the overhang of the porch, where his father, Big John Cannon, was waiting with a grim expression. The argument was not over by any means. Maybe it was the heat, Blue thought.

Every time he opened his mouth to express an idea, it seemed that his father was waiting to jump on him. They didn't see eye to eye on a lot of things, and, moreover, it was never easy to figure out what caused the difference. Studying his father's expression, Blue decided that this time he would try to hold his temper and maybe they could talk it out without any more quarreling.

Blue stopped by one of the fire barrels. For the last three weeks one of his chores had been to carry water

9

to replace the daily loss by evaporation in the barrels. "Pa, it's a little too hot to quarrel, wouldn't you say?" he began.

Big John glanced toward the corral where Blue had just saddled his roan horse. "I'm not quarreling, boy. I'm just explaining things to you."

Boy. Sometimes that was hard to take. When Uncle Buck Cannon used the word, it somehow had a different meaning from the way it struck Blue when his father used it. Big John made it sound like you were a kid who had to be told every little thing to do. It was irritating.

Blue did not answer right away. He dipped his hands in the fire barrel. The water was warm but it was cooler than the hot wind. He tossed his hat aside, lowered his head, and sloshed water over his face. That felt so good that he scooped up handfuls of it and let it run through his thick blond hair and down his neck.

"That's smart," Big John said. "You'll be hotter than ever when you start to dry." The words were measured. His eyes were squinted against the sun glare of the yard. The scorching wind ruffled the gray hair at his temples.

With his own face dripping water, Blue looked at him and held down his irritation. "I'll be cool for a minute or two, anyway." He shook his head and the water sprayed off him and hit the ground in little drops that dried instantly.

"Are you going to leave that horse standing there saddled in the sun all day?" Big John growled.

"No, Pa. I'm going to throw a few things together and start up to the lake in about ten minutes."

Because of the long drouth, which showed signs of

becoming even worse, all of the High Chaparral's cattle, except the herd on the east range, had been driven to the grassy valley near Sandy Lake. Uncle Buck and Sam and two others were at the lake, guarding the herd against Apaches and Mexican raiders.

Four men were just too few up there, and Blue's father knew it full well. When Big John didn't say anything, Blue added, "They're shorthanded up there, Pa."

Big John nodded grimly. "We're shorthanded here, too."

Vaquero, the best of all High Chaparral men in his knowledge of Apaches, was hobbling around the ranch with a twisted knee and a broken arm as a result of his horse falling in the rocks some time before. Three other riders had quit, while Klosen was in Tucson getting treated for boils.

"If something happens at the lake—" Blue began.

"Buck will take care of it. I want you here, boy."

"Why?"

"You never ask why, except so you can start an argument."

Blue's voice rose in spite of his effort to keep it down. "Just tell me why I have to stay here!"

"Because I need you."

Blue swung his arm toward the corrals. "You need me! What for? To fix corrals that don't need fixing, to fill fire barrels that never will be used, to mend saddles that—" He stopped when he saw his stepmother come into the doorway behind Big John.

Victoria was a small woman with high-piled dark hair, a beautiful woman whose expressive eyes showed her deep concern about the quarrel between two men she loved. Sometimes it came bitterly to Blue that she was not his real mother. His real mother had been killed by an Apache arrow before the Cannons were fairly settled at High Chaparral.

But he had a high respect for Victoria. She had never tried to push herself on him.

Without looking around, Big John said, "Stay out of this, Victoria."

She knew when to ignore her husband's orders and when to obey them. She made her own decision, studying the faces of the two men, and decided it was wise to say nothing at the moment.

In his slow-paced way of talking, Big John said, "Blue, you ought to know that the High Chaparral wasn't built by one great big deed, and it won't be held together that way, either. It takes a thousand mean little chores to keep things going.

"You can't seem to see that, boy. You're tired of the day-by-day work, so you want to rush off to the lake to kill about ten of Soldado's warriors, in case they try to cause trouble up there. That would be something big, now, wouldn't it?" Big John shook his head. "Buck doesn't need you up there, and I do need you here."

Except for where his hair had trapped moisture against his scalp, Blue had dried off and was hotter than ever. It made him mad to think that his father had been right about the dousing. He picked up his hat and slapped it on.

"The Apaches know how few men are guarding that herd. They could come in anytime, while I'm down here

holding the High Chaparral together with all the important little chores you mentioned."

Big John stared at him. "They just may do that, yes.
That's the chance we always take. But what makes you
think they won't strike here again, if it suits their fancy?"

"They won't. You heard Major Evans say that he
thought Soldado was way off in the mountains during the
drouth. You've always tried to make friends with the
other Chiricahuas. No, they won't come here, but up at
the lake they'll scatter that herd clean out in the desert
if they can."

"Now you're an authority on Apaches." Big John took
off his hat and ran his forearm across his forehead. "I
still can't spare you, boy. Unsaddle that horse and let's
stop jawing about the whole thing."

He was just about the most stubborn man Blue had
ever known. He always wanted his own way. Blue turned
away and stomped out into the full smash of sunlight in
the yard. He heard Victoria say something to his father
in a gentle tone and Big John growled some short reply.

Blue went straight to the short-coupled roan, getting
madder as he walked. He glanced back defiantly at his
father and then went up in the saddle.

"Blue!" Big John called.

"So long, Pa!"

Blue wheeled the horse and went out of the yard and
through the gate much too fast for the heat. He had had
enough of his father's unreasoning stubbornness. Though
he had not bothered to get even a biscuit or a piece of
jerky or extra cartridges for his rifle and pistol, he was
going to Sandy Lake.

He took one last glance over his shoulder at the house. Big John was standing in the same place. Victoria had run out into the yard. She was motioning with her hand and shouting something, but, whatever it was, it was drowned out by the pound of anger in Blue's head and the drumming of the roan's feet.

He slowed down after he crossed the first small wash beyond the house. Already the heat was a gigantic weight on him. Through sand and rocks he rode toward the hills, with the saguaro and ocotillo all around him. It was an arid, brutal land. There was not even a cloud wisp in the long-reaching great blue sky.

A good two days' ride to Sandy Lake.

With his anger seeping away, reason began to flow in. Maybe it was a little silly to go charging off against his father's orders, but still, if Big John was so determined to be hard-set in his attitude, then Blue felt he had a right to be a little stubborn himself.

At the crest of the first low range of hills he stopped to let the horse rest. It was a long way to the lake. The thing to do was to take it easy right from the first.

Looking back on the ranch house, he observed how small and lonely it appeared against the tall hill behind it and the great sweep of desert. He was not sure, but it seemed that there were two men on the roof, instead of the one guard always posted there.

The High Chaparral was a tiny outpost in a savage land. From a distance it looked the way it had when Blue first saw it, windows shattered by Apache lances, adobe walls beginning to crumble, corrals sagging—an abandoned place that the former owners could not hold against ruthless Indians and a wild land.

Yes, it had taken a thousand mean little chores to bring it to what it was today, Blue admitted. He turned away.

Ahead was shimmering distance, more vast desert running to the far mountains. The waterholes might—

He remembered then about his canteens.

They were both on the saddle, but in his haste to show that he could be as hardheaded as his father he had galloped away without filling them at the windmill tank. That was just about as stupid a trick as a man possibly could do.

He could ride back. . . . No! Pride wouldn't let him do that. About five miles beyond was a waterhole. If it proved to be dry, then he would have to turn and go back.

He rode over the crest and began the descent on the rocky trail. In spite of the smothering heat and its tendency to make one want to doze, he read the country alertly, and now and then he looked behind him.

This was Pimeria, land of the Pimas, those ancient enemies of the Apaches, but the Apaches had no more respect for such tribal boundaries than they did for the ranches of the intruding white men or the small villages of Sonora. Apaches went where they pleased. In broken country they could cover on foot more ground in a day than a White Eyes horseman could cover with a good mount.

And, as Vaquero said, when you saw absolutely no sign of them at all, that was the very time to keep your rifle in the crook of your arm, with the other hand on your scalp. That was the worst time of all.

Far, far away over the mountains that seemed to re-
cede at times in the shimmering heat Blue saw a dark
cloud bank starting to build. Sixty miles, he estimated.
Rain up there sure didn't do any good down here where
he was. Wouldn't it be something, though, to stand out in
a pouring rain just once again, feeling its cooling beat
on your head and shoulders, letting it run down over
your dusty cheeks and lips?

The dry canteens helped make it worse. And he was
barely started on his journey.

But there was a waterhole ahead.

The next one beyond that, at least the next one that
Blue knew about, was around forty miles.

An hour later he was crossing a series of long washes
where the deep sand made a dry whispering noise
against the legs of the roan. He saw three cottonwood
trees clumped together at the edge of one wash. There
was water somewhere under them, he knew, but it might
be ten feet down.

A few minutes later he saw the flash of light as he
turned to look at his backtrail. It was just a quick gleam
on a barren ridge. For one short moment he tried to tell
himself that it could have come from a piece of white
quartz up there in the rocks.

He knew better.

The flash had come from a steel mirror in the brown
hands of an Apache. Blue had passed that ridge, scanning it carefully, and he had seen nothing but cactus
and rocks. But they had watched him pass, and now they
were between him and the High Chaparral.

Sometime before, Blue had thought he was about to run out of sweat, but now he felt new perspiration breaking out all over him. He did not panic. He rode on slowly, as if he had seen nothing at all unusual.

A lot depended on chance. If that mirror-holder belonged to Soldado's band, Blue was in for it. They were mostly of the Coyote clan, and Soldado had kept them in deadly enmity with Big John Cannon. But there were other clans among the Chiricahuas who respected Big John. They did not come to supper at the High Chaparral, but at least they left the place alone, knowing John Cannon to be one White Eyes who always kept his word.

But even these almost-friendly groups had been betrayed and cheated so many times by white men that there was no certainty about their actions at any given time.

Slowly Blue went on, keyed now to a high pitch of watchfulness. He made sure that his rifle was not too tight in its scabbard. He drew his pistol casually and checked the loads.

Suddenly he was twice as thirsty as he had been before he saw that signal.

Two roadrunners scooted across his path. He saw a woodpecker working at a hole in a giant saguaro. Foam spewed from the mouth of the roan as it jerked its head and shied away from two huge rattlesnakes lying in the shade of a rock. They coiled and sounded their warning and Blue rode around them, forgetting them quickly as he continued to search out the country ahead.

To all appearances the blazing land held no other

human besides himself. The flash had been directed ahead; there was no telling how many other Apaches he had passed.

No, it was not an empty land, by any means.

The waterhole was among rocks that jutted out from the base of a high ridge. He did not go in directly to it but stayed out about a hundred yards, riding past it, and then cutting toward the hill to study the ground for tracks. There were none.

Blue circled back the way he had come and made another examination of the ground on the south side of the rocks. Again he saw no evidence that anyone had gone near the waterhole recently.

He went in to where the little basin had always held water from a steady trickle in the rocks above. Then he knew why no one had been near the place in a long time.

There was a film of feathery scum in the basin, dead-green in color, dry as a spider web. Hopefully, Blue had taken one canteen off the saddlehorn. In sudden frustration he had an urge to swing it by the strap and hurl it out on the desert.

The wild-haired devils were laughing at him. They were up there unseen on the ridges, laughing fit to kill. They had known that the waterhole was dust dry and so they had let him go to it. Nothing suited them better than to slow-pace a white man dying of thirst as he stumbled through the sand, faltering under the savage boil of the sun.

Blue resisted an urge to be gone quickly from this place that had betrayed him. He rose from the rocks and loosened the hair cinch on the horse. For fifteen minutes he stayed in the shade of the rocks, trying to think out the problem.

He could make a run for it and try to get back to the ranch. The roan had plenty of stamina. Many times it had gone much longer, and farther, without water than it had today, and so had Blue. Under ordinary circumstances, returning to the High Chaparral would have been simple.

That was just what they expected him to do, he thought. Of course they didn't know that his canteens were empty. Or did they? A few times crossing washes where the roan had to make a surging scramble at the bank, the canteens had flopped out from its shoulders.

The keen, burning dark eyes of the Apaches would not have missed a detail like that.

Blue had to believe that they expected him to try to go back, and, of course, they would be all set for that move. His other course was to make it to the next waterhole, forty miles away. And maybe it was dry, too. Involuntarily, he picked up the canteen and shook it.

Through the blanket covering he could feel the heat of the galvanized metal.

His hand left a wet mark on the strap as he put the canteen back on the saddlehorn.

A few minutes later he rode on, slowly as before, headed for the distant waterhole.

2 A Man to Ride With

ON GUARD DUTY on the roof of the house, the injured
Vaquero had heard everything going on below. Sitting
on the adobe coping, his left arm in a sling, his bad knee
paining him, he listened to the quarrel between father
and son and then watched Blue make his angry departure. He shook his head in silent disapproval.

Just before Blue reached the crest of the hill where
he would soon disappear, Big John climbed through
the trapdoor to the roof and came over to sit beside
Vaquero. Though the latter's face showed little expression, Big John gave him a hard glance and said, "Never
mind the lecture. I've heard enough from my wife already."

Vaquero shrugged. "I have nothing to say."

"Well, you're thinking plenty."

"Only a man who thinks perhaps he was a little wrong
would say that."

"I thought you didn't have anything to say."

They watched Blue reach the top of the hill and stop
to look back. The way he hesitated made them wonder if

he was considering turning back. And then he rode over the hill.

Big John was silent for several moments before saying, "Well? What do you think?"

"I think it is a very long ride he is making."

"Apaches?"

Vaquero considered the question. "In weather like this they sometimes stay in the mountains." And then he added, "But not always."

"That's not much of an answer."

"It is a good one. Who knows about Apaches?"

Big John reached down and lifted the rifle Vaquero had laid in the shade of the coping. It was almost too hot to handle. Left for long in the sun, it would have picked up enough heat to burn a man's hand.

"How about the waterholes the way he's headed?"

"Most of them will be dry, I think."

Big John put the rifle down. He looked steadily at the crest where his son had disappeared. Both Blue's canteens had bounced wildly when he rode away. Surely by now Blue was aware of the oversight. If he found the first waterhole dry and did not turn back there, he would really be biting off a big chunk to chew.

Vaquero rose suddenly and walked across the roof without limping. "My knee is good now. I can ride."

"Sit down," Big John said. The muscle knots at the corners of Vaquero's jaws had given him away; his teeth had been clenched hard while he was walking. "I couldn't spare you to go after him, even if you were able to ride."

Blue had made a decision. It was a bad one, in Big

John's opinion, but a man learned faster from his own mistakes than any other way. So let him live with what he had chosen to do, let him discover the price of foolish anger. It was a hard way to look at it, but nothing at High Chaparral was simple and easy.

Blue would have learned a few things by the time he got to Sandy Lake.

But a nagging thought kept stabbing Big John: if he gets there.

Vaquero had not given up trying to help Blue. "Manolito returned in the middle of the night?" he asked.

"He did," Big John said curtly. He had sent Manolito to Sonora to try to get some *vaqueros* from the Rancho Montoya. Don Sebastian Montoya was Big John's father-in-law, and Manolito was the son of Don Sebastian. With all the men he had on his far-flung acres, it had seemed that Don Sebastian could spare a few for a couple of weeks.

Returning late from the journey the night before, Manolito had said that Sonora, too, was in the grip of a bad drouth and that his father could not spare any men. Along with drying waterholes, Don Sebastian had Apache troubles, also.

"Perhaps Manolito—" Vaquero started to suggest.

Big John cut him off. "I'm not sending him after Blue. I want him to go to Tucson this morning to find some riders there."

"Even if they are wanted by the law, which is the case of many who loaf at the cantinas?"

"No! I don't want that kind," Big John growled. "I think Manolito can find me enough Mexican riders somewhere around Tucson. There are plenty of them."

Vaquero kept a solemn face but he smiled inside. Any Mexican riders that Manolito knew would be wanted by the law of two countries, surely. It was a brief moment of humor, and then Vaquero thought again of Blue, and that was not funny.

Through the open trapdoor to the roof Victoria had heard the conversation. Her white dress rustled as she hurried off to her brother's room where Manolito was deep in luxurious sleep, as one who deserved a rest.

She shook him roughly, without regard for his status as a deserving brother. "Wake up, Manolito! There is little time. Wake up!"

Manolito groaned, rolling on his side and pulling the sheet over his head. Victoria got the pitcher of water from the washstand. Her silence as she stood beside the bed got to him far more effectively than any rough treatment.

"What is it?" he mumbled suspiciously.

Victoria spoke sweetly. "Manolito, my beloved brother, I have something here."

"Go away."

She dribbled a little water on his back.

"Go away," he protested. "I am weary. I need a long rest."

"You deserve nothing! You did not get *vaqueros* from our father, and you came back through Tucson, and there you were half the night, charming the girls."

"I cannot help it if they find me irresistible," Manolito said, the sheet still over his head.

Victoria gave him a little more water, this time where

the sheet was tight against his side.

"Do me a great favor and go away," Manolito begged.

She splashed him lightly again. It was only a question of time, he knew, before he would get the full pitcher on him. With a sigh he rolled on his back, pulled the sheet from his face, and opened one eye. "Our father sent his love. He said nothing about you drowning his favorite son."

"You must ride, and quickly."

"That is what our father always tells me when I go home, and he points away from the hacienda. I am tired of riding." Manolito's dark hair was tousled. He had the sharp face of mischief itself. His charming, white-toothed smile made no impression on his sister.

"It is Blue," Victoria said. "He quarreled with his father and now he is gone to the lake by himself, and his canteens were empty and bouncing as he quickly rode away."

"Do me the favor of putting down that pitcher. You are making me so nervous I cannot understand your words. You were saying that Blue—"

"You heard me! He is alone on the desert, and Vaquero says the waterholes will be dry, and there are some Apaches—"

"From Sonora I rode alone past dry waterholes, and all one night I walked, leading my horse, because Apaches were close. Oh, I suffered much. Blue may suffer a little, also, but he will be all right."

Manolito started to pull the sheet over his face again, but he changed his mind quickly as Victoria raised the pitcher. "You will injure your arm, holding that great weight. Put it down and go talk to your husband."

"I will injure your head with the pitcher, if you do not get out of that bed quickly and do as I say!"

With a great suffering sigh Manolito managed to sit up. "Blue is alone on the desert, going to the lake." He blinked. "Now that I have given the matter long thought, it is not good, no?"

"No, it is not! You must dress quickly and go after him before my husband—"

"Having given the matter more thought, I think he will be all right. I did many dangerous things when I was his age, and today—" Manolito raised his hands defensively. "Wait, wait! Please be careful with that pitcher!"

"He will not be all right if you lie in bed like a fat politician while he is in great need of help! And there is little time. Before long my husband will send you to Tucson to find men."

Manolito groaned. "Work, work. . . . Does he think of nothing else, this husband of yours? I have not rested, I have not eaten, I have not—"

"Your rest is over, and I will get you something to eat while you ride, and I will fill canteens and have them ready at the kitchen door. Now get up!"

Manolito struggled to a sitting position on the edge of the bed. "My poor head is not very clear. Perhaps I will get lost in the desert and then you will have no brother and—"

"I will help clear your poor head." Victoria doused him with the full contents of the pitcher. He leaped up with a startled grunt.

Ten minutes later Big John found him in the kitchen, munching beans in a folded tortilla. "As soon as you finish eating, I want you to go to Tucson and rustle up some dependable riders, at least six. You can find that many *vaqueros* you know, can't you?"

Manolito shrugged. "I can find twenty, but some of them will be thieves, while others—"

"You know the kind of men I want. I'll leave it to you."

Manolito nodded. "I will get my horse in a few minutes." Perhaps it was a bad thing to deceive Big John, but it would be a worse thing to have Victoria angry at him for not doing as she had said.

A short time later Big John thought little of it when he saw Manolito ride around the corner of the house. Probably he was going after a handful of tortillas to munch on the way to Tucson.

But when Big John saw Manolito ride through the gate at a brisk trot, not stopping for any last minute word or instructions, with four canteens, Big John's expression tightened. He knew there was no use to shout at Manolito. All he would get in return would be a gay wave of the hand.

He watched the rider until he knew that Manolito was not going toward Tucson, and then Big John Cannon swung around and plunged into the house.

"Victoria! Victoria! I want to talk to you."

On the roof, Vaquero smiled. He seldom missed anything, not even the short flight of a bird out in the cholla, and now he knew where Manolito was headed. Though he was a rascal in many ways, Manolito was a man to ride with when things were tough.

Blue would be all right.

That was, if the Apaches were really up in the cool mountains.

3 "Amigo!"

As SURELY as he knew that the burning sun was in the sky, Blue knew that they were out there watching him, but for three hours he never caught a glimpse of anything to indicate that an Apache was within a hundred miles of him. The ridges were silent and bleak, the mesquite-studded flats dreary and sun-baked.

They liked the ridges, Apaches did; that's where they preferred to travel with their unshod horses. Even with shoes, the big roan Blue was riding was not fitted for rocky country. Anyway, he preferred to stay on more level ground as much as possible, where he had room to maneuver.

If they thought he was going to lose his head and make a race of it to the next waterhole, they were crazy. It was past noon now. He had stayed too long in the fierce heat. As soon as he could find a good place to hole up, he would stay there until nightfall.

Near the head of a sandy wash he found what seemed to be a likely spot. A lone cottonwood stood near the rocks and it would provide the shade he wanted. The ridge beyond was quite steep, with loose stones reaching all the way to the bottom. It was an unlikely route for even an Apache to try to come in on him. And there was a screen of ocotillo and prickly pear, not too dense, but still heavy enough to stop a fast-moving horse.

For the second time that day Blue looked at a cottonwood and thought of the water that had to be somewhere below it, but the dusty, drooping leaves of the tree proved that the water was now even deeper than the searching roots.

He unsaddled the roan and tied it to the tree. He found a small barrel cactus and sliced through it with his knife, gouging a hollow in the spongy interior. He had heard that if you waited long enough, some of the juice would gather there.

After a short wait, all he saw was the exposed pulp drying in the sun. He cut out chunks of it and chewed them. The taste was bitter, but there was enough moisture, along with the saliva engendered by his chewing, to take the dust from his lips and the dryness from his mouth.

With a chunk of the green pulp he wiped the mouth and nostrils of the horse. The roan did not care much for the operation, but it did eat the piece of cactus afterward.

Vaquero said an Apache could make seventy-five miles in a day on a horse, without water. Blue thought it was true, all right, but an Apache did not care what happened to the horse. He'd ride it into the ground and then eat it, if he was hungry. He could always steal another one.

Blue cared about the roan. It was going to carry him to Sandy Lake and still be in good shape when they got there.

With his rifle across his knees he sat down at the outer limit of the shade. The cottonwood was between him and the hill, and he was depending on the loose stones to warn him of any danger from that direction. By shifting position a little he could watch all other approaches.

From past experience he knew that Apaches could rise right out of the ground before you, right where you thought there was nothing but sand and sparse growth. But he told himself that, no matter how crafty they were in the ways of the desert, they were not invisible men.

If they sneaked up on you, it was because you grew careless. And he was not going to do that.

On the faraway mountains the clouds were darker and heavier now. Rain, Blue thought, actually rain up there. How he wished some of it would come sweeping in furiously where he was.

His lips were parched again and his eyes were scratchy from dust and sun. He got more pulp from the barrel cactus and chewed it slowly. It helped a little, but it was only a brief measure of relief, and then he was dreaming of a real drink of water.

He glanced at the empty canteens lying near the saddle. His pride and stubbornness had cost him rather dearly.

He felt himself drawn more and more to the distant rain clouds, those big beautiful dark masses that held water. If a great wind would rise and move them down where he was and let them drop their burden. . . . Let the center of the cooling downpour strike the small sharp gray rock beyond the screen of ocotillo.

Blue imagined water striking in a slant, splattering all over the rocks and the hot sand. He would raise his face to the sky and just stand there.

He kept moving a little, changing position enough so that his back was not exposed for any great length of time to one approach. He kept a good watch in every direction, even rising now and then to look around the cottonwood at the impossible approach on the hill.

As the afternoon wore on, with a windless, stifling heat heavy on the land, the rock beyond the ocotillo became more and more the focal point of Blue's attention. An Apache trying to worm in close would surely use that rock as cover.

Like the fin of a fish the stone was raised from the sand. A big fish with a gray fin protruding above brown water. As Blue watched, the rock seemed to glide through the water that was no longer a bleak brown, but a beautiful blue that rippled under a cool breeze.

In time it became so real that Blue thought he would rise in a few minutes and go plunge into the water.

His head drooped lower.

He roused with a start sometime later. The roan was stamping its hind feet hard to ward off flies. A quick look at the sun told Blue that he must have dozed for a half hour, perhaps longer.

It shocked him to think that he could drowse off in the midst of danger. Why, a man could lose his hair by less of a mistake than that. He studied the landscape keenly. Nothing was different. He rose and walked around the tree, ducking under the tie rope of the horse.

Pulling his damp shirt away from his body, he sat down again. Foolish as it had been, the little nap had not hurt anything. He was lucky. It was not going to happen again, however. It must have been the result of watching the gray rock, just staring at it until he was mesmerized. Well, he wouldn't do that again, you bet.

If he had only just a little water to replace some of the moisture that was being sweated out of him. It seemed incredible that he could have been so mad and upset that he had forgotten to fill his canteens. He recalled taking them from the post where a whole cluster of them hung on wooden pegs, and he had thought at the time that he would fill them just before he rode away, and then—

Canteens?

There was only one lying there by the saddle.

Both of them had been in plain sight after he unsaddled. He was sure of it. The horse must have stomped around, shaking off pesky flies, caught its foot in the strap and. . . .

He lifted the saddle. He picked up the blanket. A yellow scorpion curled its stinging tail and then slid away across the sand.

Blue looked all around. One canteen was gone.

In the sand of the wash he found two furrows, made by bare knees or perhaps the tips of moccasins of a man creeping close to the ground. As silently as smoke the Apache had come and gone through the ocotillo and other growth that had offered natural protection.

Blue's spine tingled. While he had been slumped there

asleep, an Apache had come within a few feet of him. The man could have killed him easily, but he had chosen to insult him, to terrify him, to show him how stupid and helpless he was.

For a few moments all Blue could think of was to saddle up and ride. That was wrong; that was what they wanted him to do. Nothing would suit their cruel game better than to have him running in terror, while they paced him and laughed at his plight.

He forced himself to sit down again. The next wild-haired devil that tried that trick. . . . No, they wouldn't do the same thing twice. But just in case, he tried to set up a little trap of his own.

He took a long time at it, but at last he pretended to be asleep again. Through slitted lids he scanned the wash and the land beyond. He sat that way, with lowered head, until the tension and the strain made his neck ache, and he got the uneasy feeling that someone was sneaking up behind him.

He pretended to rouse from a nap.

It was a long afternoon that wore at his nerves. If they had taunted him openly or come charging in—or had done anything at all to show themselves—he could have met the action with some of his own.

But they let the silence breed fear. No living thing challenged Blue. They were the true ghosts of the desert, ripping a man's control without ever touching him.

At sunset it seemed no cooler than at mid-afternoon, and when the sun was gone, Blue still detected no lessening in the heat. Then there was a long period of golden light that faded slowly, and after that shadows began to flow in the rocky hollows of the ridge, ever changing as the light decreased.

As the minutes dragged on toward night, Blue found it harder and harder to stay where he was. The horse grew restless, too; it knew that night was the time for desert travel.

Some horses would have given an alarm when that Apache was creeping in, Blue thought, but the roan had been the property of an Apache, for how long Blue didn't know. Sam and Vaquero had taken it from members of Soldado's band during a running fight three months before.

Well, he couldn't blame the horse; it was he who had gone to sleep, not the roan.

Night came at last. Blue rode down the wash, his rifle in the crook of his arm. He wondered why the Apache had not taken the roan. The answer seemed to be that the Indian figured he could have the horse later, along with its rider's life.

He had not gone two hundred yards when suddenly the horse stopped. In the dim light he could see its head pointed toward a clump of mesquite.

Blue jammed the rifle butt against his shoulder.

"*Amigo!*" a voice called softly.

Any Apache could speak a little Spanish. Blue sighted on the mesquite.

"Blue! *Compadre!*"

His senses were so tightly strung that even then Blue took another moment before he was sure that he recognized the voice. "Manolito?"

"Who else scratches his face on mesquite and waits

like a rabbit for hours? Who else?"

Blue let out a relieved sigh and lowered the hammer of the rifle as a dark form came from the brush and slid down into the wash.

"How did you find me?" Blue asked.

"By the simple act of following your tracks, and then by thinking as I know you think. I have been here for hours."

"If you knew where I was, why—"

"I did not go to you because it was better to give our Apache friend two different places to think about."

"You saw them?"

"I saw one Apache, quite young, I think. Now I will get my horse and we will go on to the lake." Manolito walked away before Blue could ask another question.

They were on a long flat under the starlight when Manolito passed two canteens across to Blue. "Sometimes I have left my father's house with his anger burning my coattails, but I was never so angry myself that I rode away with empty canteens."

The water was warm but Blue had never tasted better. He held himself down to a few small sips. "You saw just one Apache, Manolito?"

"I was satisfied with one. How many did you see?"

"I saw a signal. He wasn't talking to himself, was he?" Manolito laughed. "Perhaps not."

"Who sent you after me?"

"Who would you guess?" Manolito asked.

"Victoria. That's who it was."

"Shall we return to the hacienda and ask her?"

Blue took another sip of water. "No."

"As you say, *amigo*. Since I am not your father, I will not argue with you. We will go to the lake."

They skirted a stony hill and went up a slight rise where the shadowy forms of saguaro looked like tall hobgoblins with upraised arms.

"Ride on," Manolito said. "I will wait here for a while." He stopped in the shadows.

When he caught up sometime later, he said, "I heard nothing, but if they are following, they would not be caught by such a simple trick. Do you know where Skeleton Springs are?"

"No."

"It is where no water should be, and that is why it is sometimes hard to find even in the daytime. About fifteen miles from here, I think."

"Suppose we miss it."

"Then we will be very dry and so will the horses. It is a very great distance to the next water at Lobo Wash, and it is almost sure to be dry." Manolito looked over his shoulder. "Who knows, perhaps Skeleton Springs is dry, also." He seemed very cheerful about the whole thing.

A light following wind kept the dust with them as they rode. It gritted in their teeth and filled their nostrils. Blue had to exert his willpower to keep from taking deep draughts from his water supply.

He guessed that it was well past midnight when Manolito stopped and dismounted, peering through the night at a dark hill. "If you hear an owl hoot three times, bring my horse and come on in. If you hear other things, do something else."

"What else? What do you mean? Where—"

"Do that which seems best." Manolito faded into the night.

Standing beside the horses in the dark, Blue wondered what he would do if he heard nothing from Manolito. That would be the worst of all. Each little sound made him listen intently. The great loneliness of the desert seemed to run forever all around him. He began to worry as the time passed and no signal came from Manolito.

And then the owl hoots came.

Blue went toward the hill, assuming that the spring would be near the base of it. He was leading the horses, casting around in the dark at the bottom of the hill, when more owl hoots directed him away from the escarpment.

When he found Manolito he knew what the latter had meant by saying that the water was where no spring should be. It was only a tiny pocket in rocks that barely rose above the level of the ground. The horses drank greedily, emptying the small basin, and then they had to wait for it to fill again.

Manolito laughed softly. "This time you will fill your canteens, no?"

Blue was happy that the night concealed the fact that he had only one canteen besides the two that Manolito had given him. Sooner or later he would have to tell what had happened to the other one, but that could wait until the next day.

They were an hour at Skeleton Springs. As they rode away, Blue studied the land as best he could in order to fix the location firmly in his mind. "We're in pretty good shape now, Mano. We should get to the lake sometime tomorrow afternoon, huh?"

"If the Apaches do not trouble us. They, too, can travel at night."

4 The Enemy

THE NIGHT was sacred to the ancestral dead of the Apaches. Generally, they would not fight during dark hours, but now the night was dying. Blue felt the tension rising in him as the light began to break.

They had held a steady pace designed to cover distance without grinding down the horses. At dawn they reached Lobo Wash. The spring was dry. It did not matter greatly, for they still had water in their canteens. "I wouldn't have made it, except for you," Blue said.

His face gray with dust, Manolito was studying the country ahead. He was tired and on edge. "Perhaps yes, perhaps no. One can suffer much more than he thinks when it is forced on him. Give me no thanks for running away from the task your father had for me."

"You didn't have to come."

"True." Manolito kept scanning the country. "Let us not quarrel just because it is dawn. Dawn is an unhappy time. No one is full of joy then, except roosters."

Right now was the time for the Apaches to strike, if that was what they had in mind, Blue thought. He could tell by the restless movements of Manolito's eyes that he was thinking the same thing.

They rode away from the dry spring, doing their best to avoid places that were ideal for ambush. After several miles Blue's vigilance began to relax. "I think they've given us up, Mano."

"That is a thought that has taken many men to heaven in a hurry—or wherever they were intended to go." Manolito did not relax. Leading the way, he made detours to stay away from hills and rocky places that were obviously good ambush spots, and he often veered away from open spaces that offered the best passage for horses.

All this might be confusing to Apaches, who expected them to select the easiest route, Blue realized, but he was beginning to think that both he and Manolito had overestimated the Indian scare. They were only about twenty miles from Sandy Lake now, and the detours were eating up time.

Blue said nothing, but he began to fret at the delay.

They came to Coral Wash, a wide place of reddish sand and rocks that came down from the direction they wanted to go. Blue had been up it before. Manolito rode across it and started toward the plunging oak brush hills beyond.

"Wait a minute!" Blue called. "The wash is the short way, and after we get out of the sand—"

"I know it is the short way, *amigo*." Manolito rode back to the edge of the bank and looked up the wash.

"It's not half as dangerous as going through those hills. They're so thick with brush that an Apache could reach out and hit us with a short club before we knew he was even there. The wash is pretty open."

"I am not thinking of Apaches," Manolito said. "Yesterday and last night, too, it was raining on the mountains very hard, I think."

Blue was puzzled. "I saw the clouds."

"Anytime there could be water coming down the wash, more water than you have ever seen on the desert."

The sun was a heavy weight on them. There was not a cloud in the sky, and the wash was as dry as ancient dust.

"Water from the mountains?" Blue asked.

Manolito rode down into the wash. "How do you think this place was made—by Apaches with little shovels?" He took a long look at the steep hills on the right. "Yes, it will be very slow, hot work to go the long way, but—"

"The only tight place is that little canyon farther up. We can go through that in a half hour." Of course, water had run in Coral Wash at times, Blue thought, and it would again, he supposed, if a cloudburst hit from directly overhead. But the idea of water coming down all the way from the mountains just didn't seem possible.

Manolito hesitated, and then he said, "You were foolish to run away so quickly from the rancho, and I was foolish to come after you." He shrugged. "Now we can be foolish together and go up this wash. But let us hurry."

The passage began to narrow after a quarter mile, but at least they were then out of the deep sand. The way became more rocky, with a series of low, short-stepped ledges where the shoes of the horses clanged and ground as the animals scrambled up. Then they came to the short canyon, strewn with rocks. There was a dim trail that wound its way among them.

"If we had gone the other way," Blue said, "by now we'd be full of thorns and about halfway up the second hill."

He had scarcely said the words when he heard a low humming noise, a murmuring that seemed to come from all around him. He looked up at the steep canyon walls. It sounded like a million bees were buzzing around up there.

Manolito had already turned his horse and was weaving among the rocks. "Run!" he shouted.

Except for that first bit of wondering that cost him a few moments, Blue was not slow in reacting. He wheeled the roan and turned back down the canyon, following Manolito.

The buzzing grew to a shuddering noise. Blue looked back, and the scene behind him left a memory he would never forget.

For a depth of twenty feet the canyon was filled with a dirty brown rolling mass. He saw sticks and shattered trees being tossed like pine needles. It was not a wall of water, but a sloping, rumbling onrush that looked like mud. The bottom was farther back than the top, which appeared to be reaching out with hungry, curling jaws that threw creamy slobbers into the air.

One glance was enough. Blue rode for it. His only worry about the roan was keeping it from going too fast and knocking its legs off on the rocks.

Manolito looked back. Blue saw the flash of his white teeth and for just an instant thought that he was grinning, but he guessed it was more likely that Mano was saying prayers aloud.

Blue heard the grinding and bumping of rocks behind him as the water thundered through the canyon.
A thousand small washes, reaching clear back to the
mountains, had contributed their share of water from a
cloudburst miles and hours away. It was all joined now
in one terrible onrush.

The riders got clear of the canyon, and now sand flew
from the hoofs of the horses. Again, Blue took a quick
look behind him.

The water was there, all right. Sunlight struck from
high-tossed slaps of foam. But they had gained on it.
They were going to make it, Blue was sure. The crumbling banks of the wash were still too high for a horse to
scale, but about two hundred yards ahead of Manolito,
Blue could see where the wash widened. The banks there
were low. A horse could go up them in one bound.

The roan went down when its left foreleg caught in a
wedge of rock half-buried in the sand. Blue felt it going
and kicked out of the stirrups. He sailed through the air
and landed on his shoulder in the soft sand, sliding and
rolling to a stop.

He was dazed but he tried to get up immediately. His
right leg gave way and he fell. He got to his feet on the
second effort. The horse was up. It was limping away,
its foreleg dangling, broken.

Blue staggered toward the bank. He would claw his
way up it somehow. And then he saw Manolito coming
back. The horse was in mortal terror, nostrils wide, its
eyes wild, but Manolito forced it back on the dead run.

"Grab a stirrup!" he yelled, and kicked it out for Blue
to catch.

There was no time left to go back down the wash. Manolito ran the horse straight at the steep, crumbling bank. Digging with its forefeet, bunching its hindquarters in powerful surges, the animal almost made it.

The water caught them.

It was the outer edge of the flood but it was still enough. It ate the bank from under the struggling horse and then it dragged both the animal and the two men back from safety. Blue let go of the stirrup as the horse rolled over in the dirty water.

He thought Manolito was lost right there, but a moment later his dark head bobbed up and he looked at Blue with a wild, desperate, begging expression.

He could not swim, Blue knew.

As Manolito was going down for the second time, Blue got him by the hair. A tangle of tree limbs swept over them. They were tumbled over and over under the muddy water. Manolito was fighting. He tried to climb out right over Blue.

Blue never knew just what he did or how he did it. His mind was fixed on the fact that Manolito could not swim. He tried to fend off the clutching hands as they came again to the surface. Manolito had him around the neck and was still trying to climb over him.

They had barely got their lungs full of air when they were swept under again. Tangled debris struck them. Manolito suddenly went limp. He struggled no more after that.

With one hand Blue caught a floating log. With the other he kept Manolito's head above water. Alone, he could have made it quickly to the bank. But he held to his companion and kept them both afloat.

The pound of the water had diminished to a seething noise. The force of the flow decreased as the wash spread wider and wider. Trees and other debris began to catch on rocks and high spots. Blue let his legs down then. He felt bottom.

There was still a power to the water that kept bearing him downstream as he struggled toward the bank. With almost the last of his strength Blue shoved Manolito ashore, with his head and shoulders out of water. He had not drowned. He was breathing, but he was still unconscious from being struck by debris while under the churning water.

Blue collapsed facedown with his body half out of the water. He had no desire to do anything but gulp air and rest. Thankful to be alive, he lay with his head on one arm, his eyes closed.

His first act after he began to recover was to feel for his pistol. It was gone.

The roan, wherever it was now, had a broken leg. Maybe Manolito's horse had survived. Just once after the flood caught them, Blue had seen it swimming. As soon as he could gather a little more energy, he would pull Manolito up on the sand and then go look for the horse.

Things weren't too bad. They were both alive, and not too far from the lake. If he could find Manolito's horse in good shape, things wouldn't be bad at all.

He realized that his legs were getting as warm as the rest of him. Without moving his head, he opened his eyes. No wonder he was getting warm. The water had receded until both he and Manolito were clear out of it.

Blue started to rise. He got no farther than to his hands and knees. A chill ran down his spine. He was looking at stub-toed Apache moccasins, the long, high, mountain kind. Their tops were turned down below the knees. He saw bare, strong legs with the tiny white scars of countless thorn scratches.

He kept raising his head slowly. He saw a dirty breechclout, a war club, a deep chest—and then the face itself.

The long, dark hair was caught with a red flannel headband. Dark, cruel eyes studied Blue. The Apache's lips curled in a mirthless smile.

He was young, probably no more than sixteen, Blue guessed. He was already a man of powerful build, tempered to steel hardness by his desert life. Apache. The Enemy. The human tiger of the desert.

"Kanseah," the Indian said. He touched his breast with the hand that held a bow with an arrow lying along the string. He was proud of the name. In his other hand he held a canteen by the strap.

He raised it, making sure that Blue recognized it, watching with cruel amusement. It was the canteen that had disappeared while Blue slept. And then the Apache tossed the canteen aside. "Pinda-lick-o-yi," he said contemptuously. People of the White Eyes. The name for the hated white man.

Blue looked all around. Manolito's horse was standing fifty feet away. Just this one Apache. Why, it was infuriating, insulting. He had tricked Blue with that mirror flash, kept him in fear for a day and night, made him think the country was swarming with Indians.

And he had covered the same ground on foot that Blue and Manolito had ridden over, and now he was here in all his arrogance. And the flood had delivered them right into his hands.

Just one Apache named Kanseah!

Blue looked him over again.

Under the circumstances, one Apache was more than plenty.

"Chiricahua?" Blue asked.

Kanseah gave a little nod.

"Blue," the crouching man said. "High Chaparral. John Cannon. Cannon." For the life of him, Blue could not think of a single word of Apache, and even his meager Spanish had suddenly gone out of his head.

Manolito stirred. He opened his eyes and coughed. When he raised his head, Kanseah's eyes drew down to slits. "Mexicano!" Without hesitation he put the arrow to the string, bent the bow, and started to drive the shaft into Manolito's throat.

From his hands and knees position Blue scrabbled forward and grabbed at the Apache's legs. He got only one of them. Kanseah twisted away. The impact had thrown him off balance. The arrow went out into the wash, where now only a small stream of water was tailing away.

With a deft movement Kanseah snatched another arrow from a leather carrier. He was now too far from Blue to be caught by another lunge. Blue rolled over and came to a kneeling position in front of Manolito. He spread his arms wide. "No! No!"

Kanseah drew the bowstring to his ear. The arrow

now was right on Blue's chest. Until then Blue had acted impulsively, without time to be afraid. Now he was scared to death, but he returned the Apache's steady glare with half-closed eyes, trying at least to give the appearance of being unafraid.

It was only seconds, but Blue lived a long time before the tension began to leave the bow.

"Blue. Chaparral." Kanseah had slushy trouble with the *r*'s and *l*'s.

"*Si!*" Blue cried. "*Amigos!*" At least that much Spanish had come back to him.

The bowstring was no longer taut, but Kanseah's intention had not changed. He motioned for Blue to get away from Manolito. He was still going to kill him.

Apache hatred for Mexicans was as old as Coronado's time. For centuries the two peoples had murdered, betrayed, and butchered each other. Kanseah was not about to reform that ancient practice.

Blue shook his head stubbornly. With his thumb over one shoulder he indicated Manolito. "Chaparral! Chaparral!"

The Apache shook his head. Again he motioned for Blue to get out of the way.

Manolito started to rise. "Let me try him, Blue."

"Stay down!"

Manolito rose. The bow was bent all the time he talked in a mixture of Spanish and Apache. Blue caught a word now and then. Mostly he watched Kanseah's face. It did not seem to change, but slowly the tension eased off the bow.

"Chaparral?" Kanseah asked, pointing at Manolito but

he was speaking directly to Blue.

Blue nodded eagerly. Maybe his father's steady program of trying to get along with the Chiricahuas was going to help, after all.

Kanseah pointed at the ground and said something in Apache. When the two men hesitated, Blue because he did not know what was meant, the arrow snapped back on the bowstring.

"He said to sit down and look at the water," Manolito explained. "I think we will live longer if we do as he says."

Seated with their backs to Kanseah, the two captives faced the wash, where now only a dribble of water was running.

"What did you tell him a minute ago?" Blue asked.

"I said it would be a greater honor—" Manolito stopped and started to turn his head.

Kanseah's war club thumped against Manolito's skull. He slumped over. Blue tried to duck what he knew was coming but it was too late. The last he heard was the whisper of moccasins against the sand, and then white lights exploded in his head.

He woke up slowly, feeling terrible. He was lying on his side. His mouth was parched and his head was throbbing. When he tried to roll over he felt a sharp pain in his throat.

"*Amigo*, hold still!"

They were jammed back to back with a horsehair rope around their necks, so tied that when they made the least move, the rope sawed in and choked them.

"Where is he?" Blue asked.

"I don't know," Manolito croaked. "Twice now something very solid has hit my poor head. I think I will die."

"I thought he was becoming half-friendly."

Manolito grunted. "A Chiricahua?"

It was brutally hot. Their clothing was dry, encrusted with sand. Had Kanseah left them there to die? Blue wondered.

By working together carefully they managed to sit up. Except for a few small pools of water, the wash was dry, steaming in the sun at the edges of the pools. Kanseah and Manolito's horse were not in sight.

Blue saw the canteen that the Apache had tossed aside. It was about twenty feet away. By scooting through the sand they tried to reach it. They had to move at exactly the same instant, on command. Their progress was slow and painful, for each time one of them was off just a little in his movement, the hair rope bit into their throats.

The canteen was almost within their grasp when Kanseah came riding back. There was a strange bluish-gray bulge around his middle. Blue did not recognize what it was until the Apache was quite close.

It was the intestine of a horse that made the bulge. It was wrapped around his middle like a snake. He had found the roan and killed it, if it was not already dead, and now he was carrying water in the intestine. It was the Apache way, though Blue had never seen it before.

There were no canteens on the horse Kanseah was riding. They had been lost in the flood, or else he had thrown them away, disdaining them as a White Eyes luxury, as some Mexican *vaqueros* did on long rides.

Kanseah got down and made some quick adjustment of the rope. They both had tried to untie it from around their necks, but any loosening on the part of one had made the strands tighter around the other's throat, and so they had given up.

The Apache's deft unlooping left about five feet of rope between them, with the bond on their necks as tight as ever. With the free end of the rope in his hand, he mounted and started off without a word.

Manolito tried to scoop up the canteen as they went past it. Kanseah had been waiting for that move. He timed his savage tug on the rope so that Manolito and Blue were almost jerked off their feet at that point, and Manolito did not get the canteen.

They knew by the happy expression on their captor's face that if they fell, he would keep right on going, with the rope turned around the saddlehorn.

As they stumbled down into the wash, they saw all the possessions they had carried in their pockets. Kanseah had searched them while they were unconscious and found nothing that he wanted.

Among the items was a picture of a laughing, dark-eyed girl. Manolito looked down at it mournfully. "*Adios, querida.*"

5 A Glimpse of Sandy Lake

BLUE HAD THOUGHT that he was suffering from lack of water the day before, but now he quickly learned what real torture was. Without the least regard for their ability to keep up, Kanseah took them across the wash. They sank knee deep into the sand and mud, and all that kept them from being dragged was the fact that the horse also had a hard struggle to get through.

They went into the steep hills, the route that Manolito would have taken if Blue had not talked him out of it. It was too late now to waste time in vain regrets over that foolish misjudgment.

To keep from bumping into each other, or jerking the rope that ran between them, they had to keep in step. Sometimes that was impossible and then the rope sawed at their necks. It was not a slipknot, but some kind of clever tie with the knot at the back of their necks and with the rope so entwined around the first bight that the pressure always came against their throats.

Except for short periods when Kanseah stopped to look at the country ahead, Blue had no time to watch

anything but Manolito's feet. He stepped where Manolito stepped.

Blue learned the truth of what Manolito had said at
dawn that day: A man could suffer a whole lot more
than he knew, when the choice was life or death.

Kanseah gave the horse no consideration, either; it
was covered with lather and its flanks were heaving.

Scratched by thorns, gouged and whipped across the
face by branches, the captives stumbled on. Manolito
held to the rope to give them all the slack he could. Once
when Kanseah stopped to select his route, Manolito managed to get a turn around a stout limb stub.

The Apache started on and the horse was pulled sidewise to a stop. Kanseah said nothing as he came back
far enough to throw the turn off the limb stub. A moment later he kicked the horse into a plunging run
through the brush and scrub oak.

Manolito and Blue had to run until their lungs were
almost bursting. Except for a rocky wash that forced
Kanseah to stop and backtrack, the captives would have
been dragged.

Manolito did not try that little trick again.

There were times on some of the hills when they both
had to use their hands to climb. The only consolation
was that such places also slowed the horse. As for Kanseah, he showed not the least concern about the animal's
welfare, nor that of the two staggering creatures behind
it.

Out on the desert, they both would have been dead
by now, Blue was sure.

The hills they crossed grew rougher and more rocky.

At times Kanseah had to lead the horse, and it was then that the captives could catch their breath.

Blood was running with the sweat on Manolito's neck, but he mustered a smile as he turned to look at Blue. "It is an experience, eh, *compadre?*"

"I don't think I'll last," Blue gasped.

"Oh, but you will. We both will last a long, long time, if only for the pleasure of killing him. How soon that will be, I do not know, but I can wait with patience for one hundred years."

It might have been cooler among the oaks than it had been down on the desert proper, but Blue could not tell any difference. His head was pounding from the exertion and from the blow he had received. His hat was gone and twigs were tangled in his hair. Sweat running into his eyes nearly blinded him.

One sneaking, cunning, half-grown Apache, he thought bitterly. There had never been any more than that. If the dirty gut-eater had ever come out in the open, man to man. . . .

"Where would you say he's taking us?" he mumbled.

"To wherever his clan or band is."

"He wants to show us off alive, huh?"

"Yes. But take no great hope from that. Two scalps would be much easier to bring back. If he grows tired of us, or if we do not keep up—"

"We'll keep up!" Blue said.

"Good!"

When Kanseah had to lead the horse on a rough hill above a canyon, he threw the dally off the saddlehorn and let the rope lie. Blue and Manolito tried to work the knots loose, but they were as stubborn as ever.

When Kanseah came back and picked up the rope, he stared at them and growled mushy Apache at Manolito.

"He asked why didn't we try to run. He says we are a burden, and he wishes we would try to escape," Manolito explained.

As Kanseah led them away, he tried to jerk them off their feet, but Manolito had a strong grip on the rope. He laughed at the Apache.

Ages before, it now seemed, when he had been lying exhausted beside the wash, Blue had thought that the worst he and Manolito would have to face was a long walk to the lake. He knew they could do it, though it was not a pleasant prospect.

By mid-afternoon he knew how relatively simple it would have been, for now they were above the lake, high above it on a wooded ridge. Counting the ups and downs, Blue thought they must have walked well over twenty miles.

Sandy Lake made a cool sparkle. Below it, a wide, grassy valley ran for miles. Blue saw smoke from the camp in the green trees at the upper end of the lake. He saw Uncle Buck's sorrel horse in the valley where the herd was grazing.

It was all so close, and yet so far out of reach. Kanseah stopped to let them look. He laughed at their expressions.

Not that it would have helped any, but Blue thought that a loud yell could be heard down there. Even if Uncle Buck and the others had known where he and Manolito were, it would have taken them hours to come up the broken cliffs that stood above the valley.

Blue could not have shouted, anyway; his tongue was so swollen that it almost filled his mouth.

Not long afterward, it seemed that the captives were about to get their first good stroke of fortune that day. Kanseah led them up a small canyon. A spring was bubbling in the rocks at the end of it and there was a small patch of grass. The Apache dismounted and walked back to them casually.

With the swiftness of a striking rattler Kanseah kicked Manolito's feet from under him. Manolito sprawled forward in the rocks and Blue had to go with him. In a matter of seconds the Apache made his quick adjustment of the rope.

There they were again, tied closely back to back.

Kanseah beat the horse back from the spring and stretched out full-length to drink. By the time the captives scrooched up to a sitting position, the Apache was squatted at the spring, grinning. The horse came in and he let it drink. Even the strings hanging from the muzzle of the animal after it raised its head were enough to intensify Blue's thirst.

Dipping his hand in the spring, Kanseah flipped drops of shining water toward his captives. At times during the day he had drunk from the intestine. Now he took it from around his waist and swung it so that spurts of warm liquid splashed the rocks near Blue and Manolito.

Kanseah enjoyed himself immensely.

Blue could not help it. He watched the horse drinking and the water bubbling from the rocks, and a groan escaped him.

"Don't beg!" Manolito said. "Spit at him."

"Spit!" Blue croaked. "I can't even swallow."

As soon as they quit staring at the spring, the Apache grew tired of tormenting them. He sat with his back to a rock, resting in the shade with his weapons close at hand.

Cramped and aching, the captives tried to lick their lips. The sound of the spring was enough to drive them mad, but they would not look at it.

After a time Kanseah went down the narrow canyon and blocked it with brush and dead limbs to prevent the horse from wandering away. Coming back, he stopped to examine the rope. Manolito spoke to him, and for several moments they carried on a conversation.

"He says his father is Cayatano," Manolito explained. "He still thinks I am not of the High Chaparral, and that he should have killed me at the wash."

"Ask him why he took my canteen."

"Ah! I see." Manolito put the question to Kanseah, who looked at Blue as if he were a child. The answer was that it was much more difficult to take something from a man on guard than to kill him. Anyone could kill a sleeping man.

Pure bravado, Blue thought. He remembered the tales of soldiers in the adobe-walled forts of Arizona Territory. Though their sentries stood duty on the walls at night, at daylight it was not unusual to see the tracks of moccasins across the parade ground.

Like smoke the Apaches had come in the night, scaling the walls and leaving their mark to show their contempt for the White Eyes who penned themselves in tall corrals.

Kanseah stalked away to the spring and sat down,

splashing the water with his hand.

"What did you tell him at the wash when he was ready to slam that arrow into you?" Blue asked. Anything to help get his mind off that bubbling water.

"I told him it was a greater honor to bring back slaves than scalps."

"Slaves! Us?"

"Us, *amigo*. If we last long enough to become slaves. Do you know of this Cayatano?"

Blue thought he had heard his father speak of him, but he was not sure. Big John often mentioned the names of Chiricahuas, but Blue, as well as most of the others at High Chaparral, did not share much of John Cannon's hopes of being friendly with the Apaches. After today, Blue had no use for any Chiricahua. "I may have heard my father mention Cayatano, but I don't remember. Let's figure some way to escape tonight. It's not far down to the lake."

"I have wearied my poor head with that thought all afternoon," Manolito said, "but all I could think of was Conchita lying there in the wash."

"Conchita!"

"Yes! You saw her picture where this savage threw it. I thought of her and I thought of water, and now let us lie down before my back breaks."

Very carefully they eased from their sitting position to lie in the rocks. Blue was facing the spring. He closed his eyes. He wished he could speak Apache, so he could tell Kanseah a few things. It helped a little to think up a long list of expressions and insults.

The canyon wall cut the sun off early. A few degrees

of coolness crept into the narrow place. At dusk Kanseah built a small fire of cedar twigs that made little smoke. He tossed the intestine of the horse on the fire and roasted it. At ease beside the water, he ate heartily.

There was only a burned end of the intestine left by the time Kanseah had his fill. The Apache belched. He tossed the piece in his hands and then he threw it at Blue. It struck his chest and fell into the rocks. Though there was hardly anything in Blue's stomach, he almost lost what little there was.

Blue picked up the piece of meat and hurled it back at the Indian. Kanseah thought it was a fine joke. He took a long drink of water and then belched loudly. He appeared both amazed and pleased at the intensity of the sound.

Darkness came. The captives, who had been roasting all day, now felt a chill. They shivered on the uneven rocks. The firelight reached to them but the heat did not. Trying to keep his body still, Blue watched the warm brown sheen of firelight on Kanseah's chest.

He picked a spot where he would send a bullet, if the chance ever came.

Sometime later, Kanseah came over to his captives. He began to bind their wrists and ankles. Blue tried to grab his legs to upset him, hoping that Kanseah's head would strike a rock.

Kanseah stamped out of the grip and kicked Blue savagely in the stomach. It was a breath-killer. By the time Blue recovered, he was securely bound.

A few moments later the Apache drifted away into the darkness. They heard the horse cropping grass, and they heard the tormenting sound of the spring. Some-where above them a night bird called hoarsely. All else was silence.

They tried to free themselves. Since they were tied so tightly together, only one of them at a time could make the effort. First Manolito and then Blue did his best to abrade the rope by rubbing it against the rocks.

With devilish cleverness Kanseah had tied not only their hands and legs and necks, but he had looped the rope through the crook of their elbows, also, and drawn their arms back.

No matter how they struggled, they could get only very limited movement of their hands. The rocks be-came slippery with the blood from their wrists, but they could not wear the rope in two.

The fire had burned down to a dim glow by the time they gave up.

"How long does it take to die of thirst?" Blue asked.

"I have never died that way," Manolito said. "We'll find out when we get Kanseah in our position."

His grim humor helped Blue get on for the next half hour, or at least what he thought was a half hour. That was the way you had to do it, by little stretches at a time. Live through one and then tackle the next one. Some improvement had to come sooner or later.

They were half-numb with the misery of cold and strained muscles when Kanseah returned. All their senses were blunted by suffering. They did not know the Apache had come back until he began to build up the fire.

Blue stared with bloodshot eyes. He watched Kanseah

put a large chunk of unskinned meat on the fire. It was the haunch of a calf. There was only one place it could have come from: the herd down at the lake. Kanseah had gone all the way down there in the dark, killed a High Chaparral calf, and then come back up the five or six hundred feet of broken cliffs.

The feat involved skill and energy almost beyond belief. No wonder the Apaches, so few in number, still armed for the most part with primitive weapons, were truly human tigers of the desert.

And Kanseah was still only a boy in years.

Maybe he had done it as another act of bravado, as something he could brag about when he reached his father's camp. If that was so, Kanseah still was very practical. He began to eat the haunch. Blue doubted that it was cooked beyond a thorough warming.

Again Blue was amazed at the Apache's capacity for food. Kanseah ate as if he had been starving for a week.

It was the most miserable night Blue had ever known. Unable to move more than a few inches, trussed like pigs, he and Manolito lay on the rocks, while Kanseah curled up on the saddle blanket and slept like a man who had done good deeds all day.

At dawn he untied the captives, all but the rope around their necks. They could not have escaped, even if he had untied them all the way. It was agony just to move their arms and legs. It took them several minutes to get on their feet. Blue's knee was so swollen that he wondered if he could walk at all.

"We've got to do something today," Blue muttered. "Look at the dirty gut-eater chewing that meat! Maybe if we both grab rocks and throw—"

"If the very first one got him, yes," Manolito said. "Otherwise, he would have arrows in our bellies before we could throw a second one. Patience, *amigo*. Our day will come. I do not know when but it will come."

After eating like a glutton, Kanseah tossed the haunch into the bushes and took a long drink from the spring.

"Since he ate his canteen last night," Manolito mused, "we must be no more than one day from his father's camp."

Blue was exercising his knee. He was going to walk if it killed him. If he didn't walk Kanseah would kill him. "Maybe there's plenty of water from now on."

"We will see."

Kanseah saddled the horse, threw the brush blockade aside, and mounted with the rope dallied around the horn.

Blue thought he would never make the first hundred yards, but he did. It was far worse than the day before. Soon his whole existence was reduced to a stubborn watching of Manolito's feet. Living was not by half-hour stretches now, but the brief time between the lifting of one foot and then the other.

His tongue seemed too large for his mouth now. His knee hurt and his whole body cried out for relief, but he kept going. Gradually a dullness came over him, and he knew that the time was coming when his legs would quit responding.

He kept fighting, trying to delay the end, and the morning wore on into afternoon.

6 Apache Camp

BLUE NO LONGER felt any pain. He moved in a foggy world. His mind was locked on just one thing: Take another step, take another step.

They were lurching through sand when Manolito said hoarsely, "I'll hold to the rope and we'll both fall down. Get all you can before he pulls us out."

Blue heard the words and tried to make something of them. They raised a dull anger. *Get all you can*. . . . Manolito was not making sense. He was trying to divert Blue from the task of taking those steps one after another.

The splashing of water was something else unreal. Blue was in it halfway to his knees, and then it was up to his knees.

"Now!" Manolito croaked, and he fell down. Blue went with him, sprawling full-length.

They were in a river. They wallowed facedown, gulping, choking in their greediness to drink it all. Kanseah did not slow down, but the sand on the far bank gave the horse some trouble, and that granted the captives a little more time to feel the wetness.

Manolito had a death grip on the rope. Blue clung to his legs. The horse dragged them through the water and up into the sand and rocks on the far bank, and Kanseah would have seen that they were dragged even farther, except that he had to pause to find a break in the rocks beyond the bank.

They were out of the river all too soon to suit Blue. He tried to scramble back into it. On hands and knees, Manolito caught him by one ankle. Blue tried to kick free, to crawl back into the sweetness of the cool stream. For all Kanseah cared, they might have been sticks tied to his cruel rope.

But the Apache was delayed by circumstance. He had to get down to lead the horse through a break in the rocks, and that gave Manolito time to get Blue on his feet and shake some sense into him.

And then they were going again, up through the rocks and cholla, scrabbling for their lives. They sucked greedily at their wet clothing, spitting the sand from swollen lips.

Long afterward, Manolito said he thought they would have made it even if Kanseah had not been forced to cross the stream. Blue never believed that; he was always sure that the Gila River had saved their lives.

The water on their clothing soon dried. They were burning up again, and Blue was slipping back into the foggy world from which he had been temporarily lifted by the water, when Kanseah stopped the horse and gave a triumphant, high-pitched shout. Excited yells answered him.

Kanseah kicked the horse into a run. Manolito had foreseen what was going to happen and he had thrown two turns of the rope around his wrists. The captives lasted for about twenty yards before they fell exhausted. Blue hung to Manolito's legs while the horse dragged them over the grass the rest of the way into the Apache camp.

Lying on the ground, Blue no longer cared if he lived or died. Children were beating him with sticks, but he felt no pain. A huge woman put a foot against his shoulder and kicked him over on his back. He looked into her wide, scowling face for a moment, and then he closed his eyes again.

Someone threw dirt into his face, and then a rough moccasin rubbed it across his mouth.

As if from the hollowness of a great cavern came Manolito's voice. "Get up! Fight!"

Fight? Manolito must have gone crazy from the sun. Hands tugged at Blue. He opened his eyes again. Manolito was bending over him, trying to help him up. Blue made it with strength that he did not think he had. He staggered to his feet, blowing dirt from his lips, staring with blurry vision at the faces around him.

He could not tell one face from another, but he glared like a red-eyed trapped animal. He heard Manolito tell them in Spanish that they were all sons of mangy dogs.

"Yeah!" Blue muttered. "Yeah! That's what you are."

Someone struck him in the back with a limb. He heard Kanseah snarl, and after that there were no more sneaky blows.

When Blue's vision cleared, he saw about fifteen

Indians in the group around him. The camp was near the head of a grassy valley, close to a clear stream. There were eight or nine wickiups. "Ask them what clan they belong to, Mano."

Manolito started to speak, but Kanseah cut him off with a chopping signal of the hand that meant silence. He motioned for the captives to sit down. Even the smallest children, naked, beady-eyed, sturdy, were regarding Kanseah's prizes with stony, hostile stares.

They sat on the trampled ground, under the full smashing heat of the sun. Blue estimated the distance to the creek. If he could rise suddenly and get that far, it wouldn't matter how many arrows they stuck into him; at least he would die with his mouth full of water.

Manolito, too, was looking at the stream. He glanced at three brawny Apaches sitting near a wickiup. "No, *amigo,* we wouldn't get there." He turned his back to the stream.

Near one of the wickiups Blue saw a pitch-smeared willow basket with a damp spot under it where water was seeping out. He could not take his eyes from it. He started to crawl toward it. Kanseah hauled him back by the rope.

The same Apache woman who had kicked Blue on his back went to the water container and drank from it, and then, eyeing the captives with a smile, she poured the water slowly on the ground.

Blue had learned from Manolito. With blistered lips he gave the woman a crooked smile, and then he tried to laugh. It was more of a hoarse, choking sound than a laugh, but it conveyed his contempt.

A council was developing among the men. Though Blue understood few of the words, the general idea came through in the gestures and expressions. The group was trying to determine the fate of the captives.

After a time the main argument was largely between two men, Kanseah and a huge Apache who stood a good three inches taller than anyone in the group. His cheeks were pockmarked. A long scar slanted across his breast. Several times he indicated it, making some point about it.

"Is that big one Kanseah's father?" Blue asked.

"They argue like father and son, but he is Nonithian. Medicine man, I think. He wants the slow fire for us."

Blue had heard plenty about the Apache method of slow-roasting a man. They hung you by your feet with your head a few inches above a tiny fire and then they stood around and watched with high amusement as your body convulsed and jerked like a maggot on a hot rock. Eventually you couldn't swing or twist away from the slow, sure heat that drove you mad before your skull popped open.

And sometimes the women skinned a man alive while he hung above the fire.

Both Kanseah and Nonithian were angry now. It was impossible to tell who was winning.

Manolito said, "Kanseah wants to wait until Cayatano returns from hunting."

"And then they'll roast us?"

"I don't know. I'm not understanding all of it. They talk too fast."

It seemed to Blue that there must have been a great deal that Manolito had not understood, for a few minutes later the Apaches grabbed the captives and dragged them into the trees. They both tried to fight, but neither had anything left.

The medicine man had won, Blue thought. *They're going to string us up!*

Chattering happily, the Apaches put rawhide ties on his hands and ankles. They did not string him up, however. Instead, they spread-eagled him among the trees, each member tied to a separate trunk. He was suspended facedown, his stomach about a foot above the ground.

It was a back-breaker. For a short time, by bearing down with his hands, he was able to keep his backbone straight, but it was impossible to keep fighting. Blue sagged in the middle until he was bent and tortured.

Manolito was in a similar position. "Don't groan. Don't even grunt," he said. "Just live."

It was unbearable. Then the Apaches laid flat rocks on their backs. By twisting and swinging his body, Blue was able to dump the rocks to the ground. The Apaches put them back again and added more.

Every joint in Blue's body felt as if it were being torn apart. His head drooped toward the ground. Someone grabbed him by the hair and jerked it up again, and then the hand let go suddenly and Blue thought his neck was snapped. He wanted to scream out his pain, but he bit his lip and hung on.

Manolito had made no sound. If he ever cracked, Blue knew that he, too, would lose the will to live. He wondered if Pa would be proud of the way he had tried to stand up to the Apaches. Pa expected so much of him that Blue couldn't deliver, but maybe this one time he would be proud, if he knew.

Blue no longer made any effort to shake the rocks from his back. He slipped into a semistupor.

How long their ordeal lasted, neither Blue nor Manolito ever knew. They were barely conscious when someone pushed the rocks off their backs and cut them loose. They lay where they fell, until kicks from moccasined feet told them to rise.

This time it was Blue who made it first. He seemed to have no body as one unit, but rather a body in sections, each one to be raised or dragged upward by superhuman effort. But he got to his feet, weaving, his mouth open. Manolito was on his hands and knees.

As Blue stooped to help him, he fell and they both were flat on the ground again, with the Apaches kicking them.

They rose together, hanging to each other.

"Do I look as bad as you, *amigo?*" Manolito muttered.

They were hustled before a wickiup where sat a deep-chested man with grizzled hair and wrinkled face. All the burning suns and biting winters of Apacheria seemed to have left their marks on him. But he was still straight in the back and his dark eyes were keen with intelligence.

Beside him was a youth of twelve or thirteen. He stared at Manolito with the deep hatred of an Apache for a Mexican.

"I am Cayatano," the grizzled Apache said in English. He studied the captives. "You have suffered much."

They stared at him.

"My son says you have suffered well."

If there was anything good about the kind of treatment they had been getting, Blue didn't know what it was.

Nonithian started to speak in his angry, rasping voice. Without glancing toward him, Cayatano silenced him with a quiet gesture. The medicine man walked away, scowling. He limped badly, Blue observed.

After a long time of grave considering, Cayatano said, "You are of the High Chaparral?"

Blue and Manolito nodded.

"Both of you?"

"Yes," Blue said. "My friend does not stay—" His voice cracked and he had to run his tongue around his mouth before he could go on. "He doesn't stay at the ranch all the time. He comes and goes on business for my father. John Cannon is my father."

If his words had any appreciable effect on the old chief, Blue saw no evidence of it. He was glad that he had spoken the truth, for he had the feeling that Cayatano was a man to whom one must never lie.

For at least three minutes the Apache leader sat ramrod straight, in utter silence, motionless except for the penetrating dark eyes that bored into the captives. The boy beside him did the same.

And all around, the tough, lean Apache warriors waited.

Blue felt his senses beginning to spin. He did not think he could stay on his feet much longer. And then Cayatano looked at Kanseah and nodded. They must have talked it over while he and Manolito were hanging in the trees, Blue thought. The nod was the only decision he saw. And the nod determined their fate.

The waiting Apache men grunted and walked away, as if they had no further interest in the captives. Kanseah took the rope from their necks. He pointed toward a wickiup with a careless wave of his hand. It was one of the larger wickiups, belonging to the grim-jawed woman who had jeered the captives by pouring water on the ground before them.

Blue and Manolito went over to it and sprawled on the ground. The woman brought them small amounts of water in a gourd. She kept bringing it until she decided that they had drunk enough for the time being.

Their fortunes entirely changed, at least for the moment, Blue and Manolito found themselves sagging. With no longer the need to exert every fiber of their wills and bodies in a merciless struggle just to stay alive, they were so exhausted that they could not have left the camp if the Apaches had pointed the way and told them to go.

They crawled into the wickiup.

"What happens now?" Blue asked.

"Who knows? We are still alive and that is something."

They fell into the sleep of exhaustion. Several times Blue roused in a panic after bad dreams in which he was again on the desert being choked by the rope, while all around him laughing Apache women poured water from willow baskets on the hot sand. He was hot and feverish.

It had been late afternoon when Kanseah dragged them into the camp. It was mid-morning when they roused. All their hurts and aches and the full reaction from their harsh ordeal were on them with heavy force.

"I feel worse than yesterday," Blue groaned.

"I feel worse than I ever did in all my life, but let us walk with our heads high."

They crawled from the wickiup into the hot sun. When Blue got on his feet, his senses reeled and he thought he was going to plunge on his face into the cooking pit. He fought off the dizziness and looked around.

There were only a few men in evidence in the camp. Cayatano was among the horses down the valley. Women were going about their chores unhurriedly. Naked children were shouting, splashing in the creek. The boy who had sat beside Cayatano the day before was standing by a wickiup a short distance away, his expression as hostile as ever.

"There is something about that one . . . something about him . . ." Manolito said. "To the river, *amigo*."

The way his knee felt as he hobbled along beside Manolito, Blue wondered how he had ever walked on it the day before.

Carrying bow and arrows, the sharp-faced boy who had held Manolito's attention for a moment now followed the two men to the creek. They found a pool behind a screen of willows where the children were swimming, and they walked into it after removing only their boots. As he tugged his footwear off, Blue observed that the boots were run over, broken, and coming apart at the stitches. He couldn't do much more walking in them.

They wallowed in the pool. After a time they took off their clothes and threw them ashore, and then wallowed some more, letting the water soak into their skins. They washed the crusted blood and grime from their necks and wrists.

The hurts would heal but they would leave scars that Manolito and Blue would bear for the rest of their lives. At the moment, however, water was all that concerned them. Where the stream came over rocks in a small waterfall, they lay on their backs and let the cascade run over their faces.

They swallowed some of it and spurted the rest of it out of their mouths.

On the rocks above them the sharp-faced boy sat with his weapons ready. No one else in camp seemed concerned about them, but the boy watched them with an unchanging stare. When curious children came down to giggle and point at the two White Eyes, the boy ran them off with a curt command.

Sitting on the bottom of the shallow pool, Manolito poured water over his head with his hands. "I am trying to remember something. I think. . . ." Whatever it was, the thought eluded him.

"Do you think they'll let us go, Mano?"

"They have not killed us yet, and we would not make good slaves, and so—" Manolito stopped suddenly and stared at the boy on the rocks. "Heraldo?" he called sharply.

"*Sí?*" the boy answered instantly, and then he glared at Manolito and spat. He spoke no more, though Manolito asked him several questions in both Spanish and Apache.

"By all that is sacred, it is he!" Manolito said. "I recall

the story now. Five or six years ago the Navarro rancho in Sonora was raided by Apaches. All were slain but this one and two small girls who were afterward traded to the Comanches. One of the girls, I think, was ransomed by a brother of Sanchez Navarro, who dealt through the Comancheros, but this one—"

"Wait a minute!" Blue said. "That boy is an Apache, if ever I saw one. Look at his face."

"I have looked. Yesterday, before Cayatano, I saw what I saw but I was too weary to think about it. He is Heraldo Navarro, the grandson of Sanchez, whose brother restored the rancho—"

"He's Apache, Manolito!"

"You do not let me finish. He is half-Apache. Heraldo Eutemio Navarro, the son of Sanchez, both of them killed in the raid I spoke of, married an Apache girl, who had been taken as a child. This boy is the young Heraldo. You heard him answer when the name struck him like an arrow."

That was so. Blue poured water over his head, and through the screen of it falling over his face he studied the boy. He still looked one hundred percent Apache. Maybe the nose. . . . A little narrow in the cheeks, too. . . .

Manolito went on talking. It seemed to Blue that the boy Heraldo—if that was right—was following the words. Say he was thirteen. Captured when seven. Spanish would not be all wiped from his mind, probably, because the Apaches used a great deal of it. But English? It would be unusual if he had ever known any, in the first place.

"The brother of Sanchez Navarro, Refugio, has long sought Heraldo," Manolito said. "There is still a reward for finding him, though I would not claim it for giving such information, but—"

"Ask him if he wants to go back," Blue said.

"A waste of time. He is an Apache now, the favorite of Cayatano. They are father and son as surely as if Heraldo had been born to one of Cayatano's wives."

Still studying the stony-faced boy, Blue began to doubt the indications of Mexican heritage that he thought might have been there a few moments before. "Are you sure he is part Mexican?"

"One without some Mexican in him could not spit as eloquently as he did. Oh, it is Heraldo, you may be sure." Manolito nodded. "See how he looks at me. He has learned to hate Mexicans above all others."

"Then he'll never go back, huh?"

"He will go back the same way we came here, if it ever becomes known who he is. And then he will return to the Apaches as soon as he can escape. I would never try to change his way of life now. Would you?"

"I don't know," Blue said.

It would be soon enough that they would find out that their conversation had cost them their freedom. In the meantime they forgot about the boy and splashed in the water. The boy seemed to lose interest in them, too. He trotted away while they were washing their torn clothing.

They could not seem to get enough of the water. While their clothes were drying on the willows, they reveled in the pool some more.

Their status as slaves was almost settled by the time they returned to camp. Pinera, the grim-jawed woman, gave them food. She was the sister of Cayatano, she made it known to them. Blue and Manolito were ready for the food; they ate like wolves.

Manolito's memory should not have been so keen. He was right. The boy's name was Heraldo Navarro, and he had been taken in a dawn raid at the age of six. Cayatano had bought him from a Coyotero Apache for two horses, a rather high price. But Cayatano had seen something in the defiant boy that could help a great dream come true.

Nacori was his name now. From his Chiricahua father, Cayatano, he had gained a working knowledge of English. He lacked a great deal in the language, and Manolito had been speaking rapidly at times while slopping water on his face, but Nacori was telling the truth to the best of his knowledge when he went straight to Cayatano, still among the horses, and told him that Manolito and the other captive knew who he was and had talked of sending him back to Sonora.

Cayatano listened with grave countenance and then sent his son away.

Everything was changed now. The night before Cayatano had made up his mind to send the captives down to Sandy Lake with an escort. The younger one was the son of John Cannon, and Cayatano had satisfied himself that the Mexican was also of the High Chaparral.

When John Cannon had been very new in the land, Cayatano had encountered him at Ferro Springs. They had not made war simply because one was a Chiricahua and the other a White Eyes. They had camped at the water for two days, and they had talked of many things. At that first meeting Cayatano had spoken only Apache, the words being retold to John Cannon in English by one called Vaquero.

It was a good sign that Vaquero had kept the words straight, adding nothing and leaving nothing out. A man who kept liars around him was often a great liar himself. But Vaquero had spoken straight, and John Cannon had listened well.

It was a new experience to Cayatano to find a White Eyes rancher who understood that the Tinde were not all dangerous animals to be killed wherever found. Cayatano knew of only one other White Eyes who understood this—the Gray Fox, he who led the soldiers.

Cayatano had made it clear that the Chiricahuas were people like the White Eyes, having both good and bad ones among them. They were not all friends among themselves, not the Chiricahuas nor any of the other Apaches. They were much given to fighting each other at times, even as the White Eyes killed their own kind when they disagreed.

This bitterness among the Apaches which led to their warring on each other was a matter of grave concern to Cayatano. If it could not be stopped, it might in time lead to treachery that would crush all the Apaches. Of course Cayatano did not mention that to John Cannon.

They met and talked that first time and found in each other a friend.

At other times Cayatano and John Cannon had seen each other on the desert. After visiting, each had gone his way in peace afterward. Though Cayatano's clan had never raided the hacienda of John Cannon, it was true that men of his band had taken a cow for food whenever they wanted one. And they would do so again, Cayatano knew, though he had spoken against it.

Yes, Cayatano would have sent John Cannon's son and the Mexican down to the lake in safety, but now he could not do that. They had found out about Nacori. For seven years Cayatano had kept all knowledge of Nacori from the White Eyes. At first, it had been necessary to hide him when strangers were around.

And then Nacori had grown to look like an Apache, to think like an Apache—to *be* a true Apache. The soldier chief, the Gray Fox, had seen him, and the keen-eyed guides had seen him, and none of them had given him a second glance.

And then the one called Manolito had tricked him, and now it would be known who Nacori was.

The White Eyes had a great strangeness in their thinking. They believed that all those who had been captured as children from them, and from the Mexicans, must be returned. It did not matter how much the stolen ones loved their Apache fathers, or how much the Apaches loved them.

Even after many years, the White Eyes always thought it was right to take them away. And sometimes they had no families left and still that made no difference.

Cayatano thought hard about the problem. Kanseah saw him walking among the horses with bowed head and came to him and asked what the trouble was that made him stare at the ground like a White Eyes searching for gold.

Cayatano told him.

"It is no problem," Kanseah said. "We will kill them

both. No one knows where they are. The Pinda-lick-o-yi will think they were buried deeply by the sands of the flood." He glanced toward the camp, where Manolito and Blue were sitting before Pinera's wickiup, eating their fill.

"I see no problem," Kanseah said. "I will kill them now." He saw Nonithian limping toward him and his father. "Or we can wait until those who are hunting return, and then put them over the fire. We are the Tinde, and this is our land, and we can do as we please."

7 A Saddle in Coral Wash

TEN DAYS AFTER Blue had ridden away in anger, John Cannon told his wife, "Since you won't stop worrying about them, I've decided to go up to the lake myself. I'll send a message back as soon as I get there."

They were just leaving the breakfast table. Everyone else had gone out. "Thank you," Victoria said. "I will be relieved to know that they are safe."

She did not mention that there was another reason why her husband was going to the lake. With no break in the drouth, the waterholes on the west range were almost gone and the cattle there were beginning to die. Big John had finally got enough men to protect the hacienda and at the same time make the drive to Sandy Lake to save what he could of the west herd.

"You will take Vaquero?" she asked.

Big John gave her a long look. "Yes. Why'd you ask?"

"For no reason, except his health."

"He can ride. You aren't worried about that. You're thinking I want him to talk Apache. You're still thinking that something happened to Blue and Manolito—"

"Yes! I have been worried for a long time. I have had bad dreams about them."

"Dreams?" Big John shook his head, but he did not scoff. He saw how deeply Victoria was concerned.

She came around the table and put her head on his shoulder. "I cannot help it if I worry."

"I know." Big John put his arm around her. He stared at the wall. Two days before he had met an Apache on the west range and inquired about the men at the lake. The Indian said there were four men there.

Badly handicapped by having to do his talking in broken Spanish, Big John could not get the time straight with the Indian. It might have been weeks since the Apache had been at Sandy Lake. He wanted the man to come to the house with him, so Vaquero could talk to him, but the Apache would not do that.

"They're all right, Victoria. I'll send a messenger back as soon as we get there."

Big John started the drive at sundown, with Vaquero and five Mexican riders. What was left of the west-range herd was in poor condition, but they were tough Mexican cattle that had never had it very good anywhere. About half of them would make it, Vaquero estimated, and they would lose most of the calves.

It was drive to the lake or lose the whole herd.

A big brindle cow, as lean and tough as an Apache, took the lead. She had a crooked horn and an evil nature and no horse was safe close to her, but she seemed to sense where she was going. The rest of the cattle, bawling their agony of thirst or plodding listlessly, followed the brindle cow. Clouds of dust covered the riders. Their sweat washed grime from their faces into their shirts, but they joked and laughed as they rode.

Two of the Mexican cowboys had wanted to make the drive without canteens. It was the mark of a real *vaquero,* they said, to follow a herd, drinking only where the cattle drank, or not drinking at all, if that was how things were.

Big John had growled like a bear about such bravado; he saw to it that everyone took canteens.

There was one uncertain waterhole in a marshy place on the route Big John selected. They drove all night and reached it the next day, to find it almost dried up. Twenty cows and calves had already died or fallen out of the drive to die later.

Once the cattle got a sniff of the water, there was no holding them. They charged into it, trampling calves, bawling, banging horns, trying to climb over each other. In a matter of minutes they churned the waterhole into mud.

The marsh had been drying for months, so there was not too much left of it when the herd struck it, but there was enough to bog down the weakest animals. After an exhausting struggle under the furnace of the sun, the riders got the herd moving again, leaving a litter of dead and dying animals at the now-worthless waterhole.

Some of them too weak to bawl, the cattle plodded on. Calves dropped in the sand and the mothers went on, unheeding. Buzzards wheeled and waited in a brazen sky, soon to drop down to start on the eyes and hanging tongues of the dying animals left behind.

At the end of that day, only about half of the cows and

very few calves were left. Vaquero said that the mature animals that had made it that far would likely go all the way.

They drove through a second night of dust and heat with the herd drifting like gray ghosts through the cactus and chaparral. That afternoon they reached Coral Wash. The strong brindle cow plunged down into it and started up the short route to the lake.

Mud dried in thin curling chips, deep sand among the rocks, and the debris of trees from the mountains showed that the wash had run with a powerful flood some weeks before.

Having studied the sky during the drive, Vaquero said there probably had been no heavy rains on the mountains during the last few days, and so they could take a chance on Coral Wash.

The desert-wise *vaqueros* had already turned the brindle cow and were holding the herd. Big John waved at them to let the cattle go on up the wash. He spat dust from cracked lips and started to follow the herd.

When he looked back a little later, Vaquero was riding down the wash, holding to the south bank. Big John stayed where he was until Vaquero turned in the saddle and waved for him to follow.

There was not much left of the roan horse, now that the buzzards and coyotes and other scavengers of the desert had done their feasting. Sun dried scraps of hide and yellowing bones.

The saddle was Blue's.

Something had gnawed the straps in two, but the canteens were still there, tightly stoppered, and there was some water left in them. There was no rifle in the boot.

Vaquero said nothing as he kicked around the carcass. He picked up a gnawed hoof and the lower half of a foreleg with the bone broken in a spiraling pattern. Mutely he held it out for Big John to see, then he dropped it.

Beetles scurried away as Vaquero pulled at the skeleton, searching for something, anything, that would tell them more.

Big John looked out toward the flats where the water had run another half mile before spreading widely on the desert floor. "You think they—" He let the sentence die.

"I think nothing," Vaquero said. "I know this: If one had but a little warning, he could run up the side of the wash on foot."

The broken leg bone held Big John's attention. A man thrown from a running horse, with the flood pounding close upon him. . . . What chance would he have to run anywhere? And here were the remains of Blue's horse, with canteens beside them. It would seem that if Blue and Manolito had escaped the flood, they surely would have gone looking for the horse, if only to recover the canteens.

"All right," Big John said, "let's go out to the end of it and then work all the way back."

They rode slowly, far out to where the flood had thinned away, and then they came back, searching some more. Where the cattle had poured down the bank, Big John found another canteen trampled into the sand. Again, there was some water in it. He held it up, looking at Vaquero, who shook his head and shrugged.

"It was on the bank," Big John said. "That means they must have got out. Doesn't it?"

Vaquero nodded. "It would seem so."

The herd had been out of sight for a long time, around the turns of the wash. On foot now, Big John and Vaquero searched. Their feet sank deeply into the sand, and they knew that there was a greater depth of it below. Along the edges of the banks and where rocks had stemmed the flow somewhat, the sand was deep enough to hide many things, they knew, including Manolito's horse.

Big John thought of better answers than that, but none of them satisfactorily explained why there had been one partly filled canteen above flood level. After a time he said, "We'll go on to the lake."

"Perhaps if I stay and search more carefully—"

"No, Vaquero. We'll go on to the lake."

They caught up with the herd two hours later. On the way they passed calves that had given out, and a few cows standing with spraddled legs and lowered heads.

After crossing a series of low hills, they came at sundown to the lower end of the grassy valley. The brindle cow quickened the pace then, pushing on strongly, with still enough left to give a few hoarse bellows.

Buck Cannon came galloping down to meet them, his hat caught by the chin thong and riding the back of his neck, his tough bronzed face lighting up at the sight of his brother. "Well, now, Big John—"

"Where's Blue and Manolito?"

Buck's face sobered instantly. "They started up here?"

"Would I ask, if they hadn't?"

Buck shot a quick look at Vaquero, who gave a slight headshake.

"Two weeks ago they started up here," Big John said. "Have you had any of Soldado's bunch hanging around?"

Buck shook his head.

"Go ahead, Vaquero," Big John said. "Have the boys drag 'em out of the lake if they get in too far and start bogging down."

Vaquero swung his hand and went on at a trot.

John Cannon and his brother rode on to the camp in the trees at the upper end of the lake. By the time they got there, Buck had the full story. "I'd better ride down to Coral Wash and look around."

"You stay right there and take care of the cattle."

"Look, Big John, right now I don't care what happens to the cattle. I'm going—"

"Stop it!" Big John said firmly. "It won't help a thing to have you running around like a blind dog in a meat house. Vaquero and I will go back tomorrow to see if we overlooked anything. And then—"

Buck waited for him to finish. "And then what?"

"I think they got clear of the flood, Buck."

Buck grunted. "That means you think the Apaches got them."

"No, I didn't say that!"

"But that's what you're thinking. If they ain't down there under the sand, what else could have happened to them? What else but Apaches, Big John?"

"I don't know!" Big John glared at his brother. "Maybe they were dazed. Maybe they wandered off into the desert. A lot of things could have happened to them."

"Mostly Apaches," Buck growled. "I'll kill—"

"No! You're not going out on any murder spree. That's the trouble with this whole Territory right now. I won't deny the possibility that the Apaches might have had a hand in this, but every time a white man stubs his toe, there's idiots who want to go kill a dozen Apaches."

"You talk like some of those hardheaded Indian-lovers from back East," Buck growled. He stalked out of the camp and went down to the lake.

Buck thought a lot of Blue, Big John mused. It was that way sometimes: A boy could get along with his uncle better than his father. It hurt John Cannon sometimes to know that he didn't have the understanding with his son that Buck did.

The fact that made bitter gall right now was that if there had been father and son understanding, Blue, and then Manolito, would never have been in Coral Wash during the flood.

Big John thought of his promise to Victoria to send a messenger back as soon as he reached the lake. No, he would not do it; he would take the message himself— after he made another thorough study of the wash.

It was a gloomy camp that night at Sandy Lake. An overcast sky and a threat of rain did not help any. Two men stood guard, while the others slept. In spite of the fact that he was weary from the drive, Big John rose at midnight and took his turn with one of the *vaqueros*.

An hour after they went out, a furious rain began. It lasted for about two hours. If there was another cloudburst on the mountains, Big John thought gloomily,

Coral Wash would run again. He did not like to think about what the water might uncover. Or it could pile the sand even deeper. Buck had said there had been rains after the big one that must have caused the flood, and now the present one was a clincher.

There couldn't possibly be much sign left around Coral Wash. Big John wished he had let Vaquero stay there, as he had wanted to do.

Near dawn Buck and Sam came out to relieve the guard. In the chill of early morning Buck was not in a good mood. "Find any calves with their throats cut?" he grumbled.

"No," Big John said. "When did that happen?"

"Just once. The night after the big rain, an Apache came in right under our noses and butchered a calf. So don't think they haven't been around."

"They're always around. If you had made friends with them, Buck, you could have given them a cow. Then they wouldn't have had to steal it right under your nose." Big John rode back to the camp for coffee.

Buck shook his head in despair. "The way he talks sometimes. . . ."

"What do you think about Blue and Mano?" Sam asked.

"I don't know. If the Apaches got them, I'll find out." Buck stared into the vapor rising from the lake. He was not a handsome man, to start, and now his face was downright ugly with dark thoughts.

Sam was about as rugged as they come, a veteran of the Civil War, an Indian fighter, a former U.S. marshal in outlaw territory. He was a man to have beside you when things were tight and tough, but now he studied Buck's expression and said, "I wouldn't start no Indian war, unless I was pretty sure of what happened to them two. It wouldn't do High Chaparral any good, Buck."

"You talk like Big John," Buck growled. "High Chaparral, High Chaparral! That ranch isn't the greatest thing in the world, you know. When you try to stack it up alongside people you love, it ain't very big at all, not to me."

Big John had little to say to anyone during breakfast. Afterward he took Vaquero aside. "Did you talk to the four new men?"

"*Si*. They will stay." Vaquero hesitated. "That is, if I stay here also. It is not that they don't trust you, but I speak their language and we are—"

"I figured on you staying here." Big John gathered up four canteens.

"But I was going back as far as the wash with you. Even if it has rained—"

"Never mind, Vaquero. Tell Buck that I'll send up more supplies as soon as I can. It looks like we'll have to hold the herd here for a long time."

John Cannon rode away by himself. He did not go near his brother. Neither of them was in a mood to talk about Blue and Manolito, Vaquero knew. Big John would go to the wash and he would search and search, and he would find nothing. And then there would be the long, lonely ride back to High Chaparral to give the bad news to his wife. He would do everything alone because he blamed himself for what had happened to his son and to the brother of his wife.

It was not the wisest way to do things, if one wanted to grow old. The desert and the wild-haired ones who ruled it had no respect for the pride of a White Eyes, or any other man.

But Vaquero respected his *patron* for what he was doing.

From the north side of the lake Buck watched his brother riding away on a fresh horse, and he thought, "Well, there goes the old stiff-back, doing things his way, as usual." And he, too, had a great respect for Big John, even for his untiring efforts to treat Apaches as men and not animals.

But that did not mean that Buck was not going to do what he thought was necessary, in his own way.

Coral Wash had not run a second time, nor was there any evidence that the rain of the night before had reached very deeply into the earth. This far from the mountains, the downpour might have been light, John Cannon reasoned.

But he changed his mind, after he began his search along the base of the scrub oak hills. There was still some dampness in the shade, and little rivulets had run on the steep parts of the hills. Two weeks' time and now the rain. It was too much to expect that tracks would be left.

The fact remained that he and Vaquero had found the skeleton of only one horse. And there was the mystery of the canteen clear up on the bank. John Cannon searched along the hills. Later he rode slowly all around the perimeter of the flood waters. Then he walked the banks of the wash.

And then he ploughed on foot through the sands of the wash itself. He pried and pulled at piles of limbs and sticks jammed against the rocks, scattering the wood across the sand. He searched until dark and he found nothing to indicate the fate of Blue and Manolito.

He had been very close but he did not know it. Once when tramping through the dried mud chips and sand he had stepped within an inch of a crumpled picture of a laughing, dark-eyed girl. Just a small corner of it had been sticking up through the sand. The rest of it, and all the possessions that had been scattered near it, had been kicked around and punched into the wash by the trampling feet of the cattle.

The last thing that Big John wanted to believe was that the bodies of two men and a horse lay under the red sands of Coral Wash. The only evidence he had to the contrary was the partly filled canteen that had been lying on the bank.

At dark he rested a short time, and then he began the ride back to High Chaparral to face the difficult task of telling Victoria the truth. There was no saying how deep the sand was in the coves and pockets, or even in the middle of the wash.

As he rode through the hot night, his shoulders sagging, his thoughts a jumble of regret for things too late to change, Big John was not the tough, self-assured owner of a great rancho, but a man who was wondering if the struggle had been worth it.

First, his wife. An Apache arrow had caught her in the back as she turned away from a shutterless window that first night at High Chaparral. Now Blue and Manolito.

If they had got out of the flood, then it must have been Apaches. They surely would not have gone wandering off into the desert. They might have gone toward the hills, yes, perhaps because they thought another burst of water was likely in Coral Wash.

Big John wondered if he had searched deeply enough in the oak brush. A canny tracker like Vaquero could turn up things that ordinary men would never notice. But if they had gone into the hills, where were they now?

8 White Eyes

No!" Cayatano said. "I know John Cannon. I cannot kill his son. That would be wrong."

"*I* can kill him," Kanseah said. "No White Eyes is a friend of the Tinde."

Kanseah was a warrior. Cayatano was proud of him, but there was a danger sometimes when a person always thought in the straight and simple terms of a warrior. There were too many Pinda-lick-o-yi in the land now, with more always coming, for the old ways to be the answer to everything.

Kanseah looked at the medicine man coming toward them. "Nonithian wishes to kill them, too."

Cayatano looked with grim disfavor on the medicine man. Nonithian was much too vain about that scar on his chest which a Mexican long knife had given him that time when the band was surprised by soldiers. One or two good fights did not make a great warrior.

"If they are not killed, they will give us great trouble always," Kanseah said. "Word of them will get to the White Eyes and then there will be soldiers after us. The

Gray Fox with those who ride forever on the mules will follow us wherever we go."

That was true, Cayatano had to admit. "And if we kill them, you think he will not follow us?"

"Who will know? They were drowned in the flood and now lie deep beneath the sand." Kanseah smiled. "If they live, Soldado will hear of them, too, and that will be more trouble than a hundred White Eyes."

Nonithian stopped a short distance away. He looked at the sky. He could see things there that no one else could see and he was fond of making a great show of his ability.

What Kanseah had said about Soldado was true, Cayatano thought. Kanseah and Soldado had a common belief: The Pinda-lick-o-yi could be driven from the land forever. Cayatano looked up the green valley, remembering faraway days when there had been very few White Eyes. It was so; life had been better then. It was enough then to win over the desert, to fight the Pimas and the Papagoes, and, when necessary, other Chiricahuas of different clans.

But now, the thing that Kanseah and others like him could not understand was that the Pinda-lick-o-yi were in the land to stay. It was true that the Apaches had killed many of them and would kill many more, but the White Eyes would never be driven out.

It had been Cayatano's hope that his sons would understand that someday the Apaches would have to live in peace with the White Eyes. Yotavo, the oldest, had just begun to grasp the teachings of Cayatano when he had been killed in that same fight with Mexican soldiers in which Nonithian received his important scar. And Nano had died in a fight with Comanches during one of those times when no one knew that the Comanches were not at peace with the Apaches.

Kanseah had never understood. All he knew was war, and that was no longer enough for great leadership. He had respected his father's teachings just enough to bring the captives into camp instead of killing them. It must have been a great effort for him to do that, but still he did not understand.

Nacori was the hope. Before Cayatano took the long ride from which there was no returning, his dream was to teach Nacori how to put his feet on the path that would make him a leader who would bring peace and honor to the Apaches.

It would take a long time, surely, and there would always be a few wild ones like Soldado who thought that the old ways could win. It was a big dream and Cayatano knew he would never live to see it happen, but Nacori had many years to work it out. Already he had shown great promise. He still nourished a deep hatred of Mexicans, but even that might be tempered in time.

Kanseah grew restless during his father's long silence. "Shall I kill them now?"

Cayatano studied his son quietly. "Why did you not kill them at the flood, or afterward?"

"One was of the Chaparral, which you do not want harmed. He was very brave in standing before the Mexican, whom I was going to kill, and then the Mexican said it would be a greater deed to bring them here as captives, and that was true. Now they are here and it is time to kill them." He shifted his feet.

Having found some great revelation in the sky, while overhearing the conversation, Nonithian came limping up. "Your son speaks truth."

"He speaks foolishness," Cayatano said. "He sees only today and nothing of tomorrow."

"I can see tomorrow," Nonithian said. "It came to me in a dream last night. The Gray Fox was after us with his soldiers, and with him were Chiricahua scouts who knew all our trails and secret hiding places. . . ." Once started, his dream had a very long tail.

Cayatano was forced to hear him out. A medicine man, even though he spoke of dreams he had in the night, which were the same as thoughts he had had before he dreamed, must be respected.

It seemed that Nonithian had told everything, but he was not yet finished. "And just a moment ago, I saw in the sky an eagle doing strange things. It meant that Soldado was after our captives so that he could sell them back to their people for guns. . . ."

Great warrior though he was, Kanseah was afraid to look at the sky for fear it would show disrespect to the medicine man. Cayatano looked. He saw no eagle. Of course, there might have been one a few moments before.

Nonithian went on and on, polishing his speech to be repeated later to a larger audience. He ended by saying, "To escape all this badness, we must kill them over the fire."

Cayatano shook his head. He was still the chief of the Wormwood clan, his position solid because of the respect of his people. His word would stand. Nonithian did not dare to take his challenge too far.

Nonithian glanced at Nacori, who was standing by a wickiup, watching the captives. "Then free them," the medicine man said slyly. "Perhaps they will promise to say nothing to the White Eyes soldiers about Nacori."

Kanseah laughed scornfully. "That is what they would say, if they thought it would free them. Like all the White Eyes, they would lie."

"I do not think these two would tell that lie," Cayatano said.

"Ask them!" Nonithian said. "Let us hear their lie, and that will tell us what to do with them."

Cayatano was in a bad position. He was known among all Chiricahuas as a man who dealt harshly with liars. Now his own son and the clever medicine man had edged him into a corner.

He met the challenge without hesitation. "I will ask the question."

Blue and Manolito were still eating when the three men walked up to them. "I don't like the looks of this," Manolito muttered.

"If I free you, will you promise to say nothing of the one you called Heraldo?" Cayatano spoke in English. Nonithian objected angrily, since he knew very little of the language. Cayatano then repeated the question in Apache.

Kanseah stepped quickly between the two captives to prevent them from conferring either by looks or gestures.

Manolito gave the old chief a steady stare and shook his head slowly. "I will not promise that." He had read the situation correctly. He knew it was no time for a lie.

Cayatano pointed at Blue.

It never even occurred to Blue to try to deceive the stern old Apache. "I will not promise," he said, and Manolito translated the words into Apache.

Even Nonithian was slightly impressed. He had been sure that the two White Eyes would jump to a lie. All of them were liars, in his opinion. Though it was strange that these two should speak with straight tongues, it did not greatly change his ideas about them.

Cayatano's face was stony, but he was pleased that the captives had been honest. He looked at Kanseah. "We will leave this camp now. We will go far into the mountains and I will think about what must be done."

Kanseah was fingering his knife. "And these two?"

"They will go, too. They will be slaves." It was the best Cayatano could do for them. Perhaps in time they would change their minds about Nacori.

"What did he say, Mano?" Blue asked anxiously.

"He said that you and I have just been hired to do the work of women." Manolito laughed. "No money, *amigo*, but we are going where it is cool."

"If they think I'm going to be a—"

"I think we both will, if we want to stay alive."

Though the hunters were still out, the camp began to move at once. Young boys raced down the valley and brought in the horses. There were no tents or other heavy gear to take down and pack. The wickiups were simple brush shelters, some with blankets or scraps of canvas thrown over the brush.

Cooking utensils were few. Blue had known that

Apaches always traveled light, but this was the first time
he had even seen them move a camp. Pinera gave him
orders, by shouts that he did not understand and by
gestures that he could partly understand.

He saddled horses. He picked up the gear she indicated. She bossed him thoroughly. Blue looked at the
grinning Manolito, who was getting the same treatment
from another woman. At least Mano could talk back to
her in Apache. All Blue could do was try to obey orders.
Sometimes when Pinera couldn't make him understand
readily, she gave him a kick.

She had a strong leg and a big foot.

What a miserable thing it would be if Buck and Sam
and the others found out that he had been booted around
by an Apache woman!

Manolito laughed at his expression, and after a time
Blue found some humor in the situation himself. And being a slave was some better than being suspended in the
trees by the ankles and wrists, with rocks on the back.

It took no more than fifteen minutes to get the camp
on the move. The men and the women rode, with the
younger children seated behind their mothers. There
were four babies in cradleboards. The older children
trotted along on foot.

At first, Manolito and Blue were in the middle of the
procession, but gradually they fell back until they were
behind the last horse. And behind them, on foot, came
Kanseah and Nacori, both appearing to be hopeful that
the captives would try to escape.

At a pace that soon had Manolito and Blue panting,
the Apaches went up and up, winding their way through

rocks where there seemed to be no passage.

Once more Blue and Manolito found themselves exerting every effort to keep up. This time there was no rope around their necks. There would be, Kanseah told them, if they faltered.

"How do these savages do it?" Blue gasped.

"Outdoor living," Manolito said. "Plenty of rotten meat, rats, and roasted guts—"

"Shut up!" Blue had eaten far too much and now he knew it. He hoped he could hold it down and keep going. It wouldn't be too long before Pa or Uncle Buck would be looking for him and Mano. The first time a High Chaparral rider saw all those things that Kanseah had taken from their pockets and thrown into Coral Wash, the story would be fairly clear.

In the afternoon one of Blue's boot soles came loose. At every other step it flopped back, and then he would come down on his foot, with only the sock to protect it. The sock did not last long. When the Apaches stopped to get a report from the scouts, he tore one arm off his shirt and bound it around the loose boot sole.

A half hour later the shirt was a worn rag lying in the rocks. Nacori threw a piece of rawhide lacing at him. That lasted longer than the shirt, but it soon wore through, and when the party stopped that evening in a high valley Blue was hobbling on a bloody foot with the spines of cactus embedded in it.

He and Manolito were put to work at once, unsaddling the horses, carrying gear, gathering firewood. The hunters had caught up with the party long before and now there was deer meat roasting on the fires, hide and all.

After everyone else had eaten, the women tossed scraps of meat to the captives.

Shaking dirt from a bone with some meat still left on it, Blue asked Manolito, "How long do you think it will be before someone knows about us?"

Manolito, too, was gnawing on a bone like a dog. He spat pine needles away and shrugged. "It might be a very long time, *amigo*. What we must do now is to become Apaches."

Blue looked around the camp. Brown bodies gleaming in the firelight. Meat half-cooked, with the hide still on it. No wickiups tonight, so they would probably be on the move again at daylight. Become like them? Manolito must be out of his head to think that it could happen.

But Blue gnawed the half-cooked meat, spitting out some of the dirt that ground against his teeth.

Back in the shadows, the ever-watchful Nacori, always carrying his weapons, sat in silence with his eyes on the captives. Manolito turned to look at him casually before stretching out on the ground with a sigh. After a time Manolito said, "That slender one by the middle fire is not bad to look at, eh?"

Blue was trying to pick thorns from his feet with a sharp rock splinter. He threw a startled glance at the Apache girl called Chema. Maybe she would look good to an Apache, but she did not look very good to Blue. "You'd better not have anything to do with her, Mano!"

"Perhaps I will marry her and settle down to the good life of an Apache," Manolito teased.

A moment later Pinera came over and kicked him up to get more firewood. Manolito sighed and began to gather sticks. "I have changed my mind about marrying an Apache woman."

Kanseah roused the camp in the cold of early morning. Obviously he was anxious to get as far away as possible from Sandy Lake, or any other contact with the Pinda-lick-o-yi. Again, Blue and Manolito did women's chores. Just before the Apaches moved out, Pinera dug into a leather sack and tossed Blue a pair of high moccasins.

He gave her a startled look of thanks. She scowled at him and turned away.

The moccasins were too large but Blue was very grateful for their protection. Thorns and cactus spines in his feet still pained him, but after what he had been through, he was beginning to accept such minor discomforts.

For three more days Cayatano led his people farther into the mountains. Travel was not so rapid now; sometimes there were delays of an hour or more while the main party waited for scouts to come in and report. Blue and Manolito knew by the sun that the general direction they were going was north, though they made frequent detours to the east or west to avoid something the scouts had seen.

It seemed that Cayatano wanted no encounters with anyone at all, not even his own tribesmen.

They were somewhere in the Mazatal Mountains, Manolito guessed. He had never been there before, but he had heard that there was a great canyon with a river in it, and he thought that it was not far away.

The Apaches did not go that far. After a hazardous descent of a trail that made Blue sick at his stomach, they came to a small, tight-walled canyon with a clear stream. Grass and willows grew beside it, and there were caves in the undercut red rock.

When the captives were ordered to help build wicki-ups, they knew that the Apaches planned to stay for a while.

Manolito's boots were almost gone and his clothing was torn, but still he had enough to cover him. It was not so with Blue. He had torn the sleeves from his shirt when he was trying to keep the loose boot sole from flopping, and he had ripped the seams in his pants wide open while scrambling over rocks.

The Apaches thought it was very funny, but he did not. He used what was left of his shirt to make a breech-clout. He kept his belt around his bare middle because it might prove a useful piece of leather, if the Apaches ever let him have anything to hang on it.

After saving their lives, Cayatano had ignored them. Kanseah tried to pretend they did not exist, but now and then Manolito and Blue saw him watching them with a curious expression, as if he could not understand how two White Eyes had lasted so long.

Nacori, too, seemed puzzled. In unguarded moments his look of utter hostility softened as he watched Manolito going about his work, joking with the women, acting like a man who was happy to be where he was. Occasionally Manolito tried to trap him with a casual question in Spanish.

It worked twice, and both times Nacori turned away in anger.

Vigilance over the captives had relaxed somewhat.

Aware of the remoteness of the canyon, Blue could understand why the Apaches considered escape unlikely. He knew, also, that there was always a guard on the trail. And a few glances at the towering walls of the canyon were enough to squelch any idea of a hasty departure by that route. He and Manolito belonged to the Apaches.

9 Vaquero and Buck

THE TRAIL was old. And now there had been two severe rains to make tracking almost impossible. But Vaquero was a patient man who missed very little. Now and then he found an overturned rock or the vague outline of a hoof mark as he and Buck Cannon went slowly through the hills.

By the condition of the drying leaves on the broken twigs, Vaquero estimated that the horse had gone through the oak brush thickets on the plunging hills about the time of the flood in Coral Wash.

On the second day he found gouges on a rocky ledge, and he said they had been made by a shod horse. He took a few strands of sorrel hair from a limb stub and studied them as he held them between thumb and forefinger.

Buck squinted at the evidence. "That ought to be enough to prove it. Manolito's horse went through here, and somebody was riding him."

Vaquero nodded. "Apache." They had led their own horses almost all the way during the search, and there had been places where no white man would have gone, unless he was desperate to escape something.

In two places Vaquero had seen shallow marks that might have been footprints of someone walking behind the horse, but they had been so indistinct that one could not be sure. From hard experience Vaquero had learned the danger of jumping to a conclusion just because one wanted to believe it.

Guessing at the nature of tracks had proved fatal to men Vaquero had known. He would make no guesses on the basis of unclear evidence.

Buck showed more patience than Vaquero expected. It took three days to come to a narrow canyon where someone had camped beside a bubbling spring. Vaquero pointed out the fact that the grass in the small crevices of the rocks had been cropped short.

"We know there was a horse," Buck said, "and we're pretty sure an Apache rode it. Find something to prove that Blue and Manolito were here."

Vaquero did his best. In the rocks where the rats had dragged it, he found the gnawed bone from the haunch of a calf, and he found pieces of hide to prove the color of it. He even found bits of dark horse hair on a sloping rock where the rain had washed them into a crack.

"Hair rope, maybe," he said. "Perhaps from a hair cinch, if he dumped the saddle here."

"Manolito didn't have a hair rope."

"No. But the cinch of his saddle was made of hair, and it was dark."

Buck sat down on a rock. "You're saying they weren't here. You're saying they drowned in that flood!"

"Easy, *amigo*. I am saying nothing, except to tell what I find." Vaquero had not mentioned the shallow marks that might have been boot tracks. He would raise no false hopes.

"We'll stay with the trail, if it takes us to Texas," Buck said. "I say the Apaches got them!"

That was what he wanted to believe. To think otherwise was to say that Blue and Manolito were dead. Again Vaquero withheld a thought: If the Apaches had got the two, the chances of their being still alive were very poor. "I will go as long as you wish."

"If we trail like this, we'll be all the rest of the summer getting anywhere. We've got to find them fast, Vaquero. Where would an Apache go from here?"

"You ask that?" Vaquero spread his hands.

"If he had captives, he'd go back to his camp, wouldn't he?"

After a moment Vaquero nodded.

"All right! Now, where's the closest rancheria of those brown devils?"

Vaquero grunted. He put his bad leg up on a rock to ease it as he stood in frowning thought. "The nearest rancheria is far up the Gila. That is, the nearest one that I know of. It is a long way."

"That doesn't matter. Let's head for it."

Vaquero was not enthusiastic about the plan. "That is one way to find Apaches," he said slowly. "Perhaps in great numbers, and perhaps the wrong ones, too."

Buck was already going toward his horse. "What's your way?"

"To go slowly." Vaquero pointed at the firesite. "To

be sure where this one was headed. In less than one day we can tell whether he is going up the Gila, or in some other direction. There are many fine camping places where small bands of Apaches go every summer, and some of these I know."

Buck held down his growing impatience. "All right, let's trail for one more day."

That afternoon they crossed the Gila at almost the same place where Blue and Manolito had drunk water while being dragged. Beyond the far bank Vaquero found scored rocks to indicate that a horse had passed through a rocky gap.

"If he had been going to the rancheria, he would have stayed on the other bank for a half mile," Vaquero said. He hesitated, not liking to abandon the trail and to go on by guess, but at last he said, "Now we can ride. I know where there is a favorite camping place not far into the hills from here."

If he missed, it would mean returning to the river to begin the painstaking task of tracking all over again.

At sundown they reached a deserted Apache camp in a grassy valley. Wickiups still stood in good condition, like brushy beehives. Ponies had foraged on the grass, but now it was coming back strongly. Vaquero dismounted and crushed pieces of horse manure with his heel, trying to read the age of them from their dryness.

"Because of the rain it is hard to tell," he said. "Perhaps three weeks ago. From the looks of the grass, too, I would say it was about then."

They explored the camp carefully. Part of a blanket, an arrow, a corn jar, and a broken knife had been left behind. The two men crawled in and out of the wickiups, seeking some sign that two captives had been held in the camp.

Vaquero spent a long time kneeling among the trees beyond the wickiups. Someone had carried flat rocks from the hill and left them strewn carelessly on the ground. He found three trees with pieces of rawhide tied to them. It had been cut with a knife.

It might be, he thought, that someone had been tied to the trees while in a sitting position, but the pieces of rawhide were far apart, as if three people had been tied.

He was lying on the ground, his legs spread wide, his arms outstretched, when Buck came into the trees. Buck stared at him with a puzzled expression. Vaquero shifted his position, still prostrate, reaching out for two trees, and then he got on his hands and knees and peered intently at the trunks of the two trees.

He rose and nodded with a grim expression.

"What is it?" Buck asked.

"The Apaches have many ways of torture. This is one that I could not remember for a time, but now I do." He explained about the practice of tying a victim by hands and ankles to four trees, with rocks upon his back.

"They were here!" Buck cried. "Blue and Manolito were here!"

"Two people were tied here, I think," Vaquero said carefully. "Sometimes Apaches do this to each other, so I do not say who was tied here."

"It figures out right! We trailed the Apache all the way here. The time checks out, and the fact that two men were tortured—" Buck stopped suddenly. "How many men live through that kind of thing?"

Vaquero spread his hands. "How long did it go on? And who can say what any man can stand? Manolito is very tough." He let it stand there.

"You don't think Blue is, huh?"

"Once I saw Manolito tied to a saguaro by *bandidos* who wanted him to tell them something he would not tell. His back was against the cactus, and, when he kept laughing at them, one pulled the rope tighter until he was almost part of the saguaro itself.

"It was one time when Mexican soldiers arrived not too late to be useful. It was one time when I was happy to see them. Yes, I know how tough Manolito is."

"Where were you while all this was going on?" Buck asked.

"I was tied to another cactus," Vaquero said simply. "I cursed them to keep from screaming, but Manolito laughed at them." He waved his hand at the trees. "And that is why I say that if the Apaches had him here, he would have given them little pleasure with his laughing."

"Who else but him and Blue would have been here?" Buck demanded. "I say it had to be them!"

Vaquero spoke slowly. "If they were here, and lived, then they were taken away. If they did not live. . . ."

"Yeah. Let's look around."

They made a thorough search beyond the limits of the camp. It was dusk when they quit. "It is strange for the Apaches to keep captives who are already grown men," Vaquero said.

"Ransom?" Buck asked.

"It is not impossible. Soldado might do such a thing,

but if he had Blue and Manolito, he would be quick to send word to the High Chaparral, and there has been no word."

Buck unsaddled his horse and sat down beside one of the cold firesites. What Vaquero had just said was a disturbing fact, and the complete lack of any proof that Blue and Manolito had even got out of Coral Wash bore more heavily on him than he cared to admit. That canteen that Big John had found on the bank really did not mean a thing. The Apache who had taken Manolito's horse could have thrown it there.

But Buck Cannon would not quit as long as there was any hope that Blue and Manolito were still alive. "Are you willing to go on in the morning?"

Vaquero nodded.

They built no fire that night. At first Buck refused to sleep in one of the wickiups, but about midnight, when Vaquero relieved him at guard, Buck forgot his scruples and crawled into the shelter.

Resuming the slow business of following a cold trail the next day, Vaquero pointed out the fact that the Apaches apparently had expected no pursuit, for they had traveled in one body.

He made their first important find when the light was beginning to fade. On a rocky hill he found the sleeve of a woolen shirt. Except for the heavy seam, it had been worn in two at the elbow.

"That's Blue's shirt!" Buck cried.

Vaquero turned the rag carefully in his hands. "He had one like this, true." He did not add that probably a hundred men had bought similar shirts in Tucson.

Buck, however, was convinced beyond any doubt that the sleeve had been Blue's. He put the sleeve in his saddlebag, as if possession of it would help sustain his hope.

They made a dry camp in the rocks and talked it over. They could go back to Sandy Lake for help, or they could go on until they had indisputable evidence that Blue and Manolito were alive.

"And then?" Vaquero asked. "There are, I think, about twenty-five Apaches in this bunch we are following, and they may be going to a big rancheria where there are a hundred more."

"You want to turn back, just when we're on a hot trail?"

"I will go on," Vaquero said. "It is not a very hot trail, as you say, and it will be less hot after the rain, which is sure to come again on these mountains, but I am willing to go on."

He did not ask what Buck intended to do if they did find Blue and Manolito in an Apache camp. There was no need to ask, for he was sure that Buck did not know himself, and neither did Vaquero. They would have to face that when, and if, they ever found the captives.

The next morning they worked with their heavy knives to pull the shoes from the horses. Shod horses were all right for the cavalry, or any large body of riders who did not care how much noise they made. But Vaquero and Buck were only two, intruders deep in Apache land.

Though they would have to go even slower now to keep from laming their mounts, they would make less noise. Their dried meat, jerky, was nearly gone. They saw deer and other game, but to fire a rifle was to invite curious visitors they did not need. Vaquero said they would have to live like Apaches from now on, even if it came to eating rats that they could poke out of brush piles.

"Whatever it takes, that's what we'll do," Buck said grimly.

The weeks-old trail became more difficult to follow. While it had been headed steadily north, it suddenly veered to the west, going crosswise through the drainage run. It would have been much easier to go with the ridges, Vaquero said. Though there was no evidence that the Apaches had been fleeing in haste, they had been avoiding the natural routes.

Buck took this as a good sign. "They've got our boys, and they don't want any other Apaches to know it."

Vaquero did not argue the point, though he could not follow the reasoning.

Buck's contention seemed to be borne out when they found Blue's boots at a campsite.

They were badly worn, with one of the soles loose back to the instep. Buck held the footwear up by the straps. "Look at them! He's walked every inch of the way. His boots were almost brand-new, remember?"

"So has Manolito, if he came with them."

"He was here," Buck said confidently. "One of these days we're going to get close enough to find his tracks in one of these camps."

Vaquero nodded gloomily. "I hope so."

Buck put his hand on Vaquero's shoulder. "I know, *amigo*. Because he's a Mexican, you think the Apaches would kill him quicker than they would Blue, maybe."

"I am sure of it."

"They haven't, though, or else we'd have found him. Doesn't that make sense?"

"There is a little hope in it," Vaquero said.

He lost the trail the next day. It suddenly turned east in another confusing move. The fresher marks of unshod ponies crossed it. Manolito's shod horse had been the major factor in holding Vaquero to the trail, but now it seemed that its rider must have pulled the shoes.

Vaquero cast around all day. He used every trick and skill he possessed to pick up the sign, but when he and Buck made dry camp that evening among the cedars and piñons, Vaquero said they would now have to proceed by guesswork.

"Where did it seem they were headed?" Buck asked.

"I thought toward the great canyon of the Salt River, until they kept turning aside from it so many times. Now I can only guess."

"All right, let's go to your big canyon. I've always wanted to see it, anyway."

That was the night they lost their horses. It rained while Buck was on guard in the early morning hours. The horses were picketed in a small opening where sparse bunch grass grew. Buck had quietly changed his position several times. During the worst of the rain he had moved back under the partial protection of a big piñon.

He was not dozing. He heard his horse snort and stamp its feet as it veered around at the end of its rope. Moments later both animals were gone and a triumphant

Apache yell rose in the semilight. Buck had not even seen anything to shoot at.

Vaquero read the sign at daylight. One Apache. He had not even crawled. Keeping one horse between him and the guard position, he had walked in boldly, cut the picket ropes, and made his getaway.

Buck looked around at the broken country. Hills, draws with sandy bottoms, and ravines of tangled growth. "Well, they know we're here," he said.

"They have known it for many days. How are your boots, *amigo?*"

"To tell the truth, they're not much good."

Vaquero sighed. "I had thought to buy a new pair when we were last in Tucson, but there was a girl in this cantina. . . . Now we both must grow tough feet."

"You and the girl?" Buck grinned.

Vaquero laughed.

They cached their saddles and bridles on the limbs of piñon trees, on the remote chance that someday they might pass by the place with horses.

The Apache who had stolen their mounts had gone south. They walked north, heading toward the great canyon.

If fortunes of war could be bad, they could also be good. Footsore and weary from unaccustomed walking, they reconnoitered from a wooded ridge in the middle of the afternoon. Coming toward them on a lower ridge was a lone Indian rider with a packhorse. Vaquero gave Buck a wicked nod and pointed across to a place where the rider would likely pass.

They sneaked down from their ridge, crossed a small

canyon, and set their ambush.

It was an Apache. He seemed more concerned with what lay behind him than what was ahead. He rode between them. Vaquero stepped out from the left side. He called for the Apache to stop. The man slid to the offside of his horse and tried to make a run for it.

Buck killed the animal with a shot through the neck. The rider took a rolling spill and came up like a cat, tugging at a pistol in his belt. The excited packhorse overran the dead mount and crashed into the Apache an instant before Buck would have killed him.

Though partly dazed from the impact, with his pistol knocked from his hand, the Indian tried to scramble away into the trees. Vaquero leaped down the hill and knocked him out with his rifle barrel.

While Vaquero was tying the Indian's hands to his ankles, Buck went through the packs. It was a strange mixture of loot: Comanche bullhide shields, bows and arrows, three needle guns with A.T. stamped on the stocks, cartridges in buckskin sacks, plugs of tobacco, sugar, several yards of red flannel, some Navajo blankets, and other items.

By the time Buck finished ransacking the packs, Vaquero was questioning the sullen captive. The man's eyes kept darting suspiciously toward his backtrail. He talked readily.

"I promised we'd let him go if he told the truth," Vaquero said.

"The truth! Him? That's a fat chance."

Vaquero pressed on with his questioning.

"He's one of a small bunch of Chiricahuas that raided

an Arivaipa camp while all the men were away. They looted it and then they scattered and headed back toward the desert. He says he doesn't know anything about any captives."

Buck fingered his rifle. "He's lying!"

"I don't think so. His raiding party has been out for more than a month, clear into Navajo country. They didn't have any luck up there and they were on their way back when they hit the Arivaipa camp." Vaquero sent several more sharp inquiries at the Apache, who shook his head. "I'm sure he knows nothing about Blue and Mano."

Vaquero stepped over to the Indian and began to untie him.

"Wait a minute!" Buck protested, but Vaquero went on with his work. Freed, the Apache scrambled into the trees and was gone in a matter of seconds.

"Now, why'd you want to do that?" Buck asked. "He'll be back tonight and steal our horse!"

Vaquero shook his head. He looked down the ridge. "He will not waste time, and I do not think we should stay here any longer, either."

The loot from the packs was scattered on the ground. Vaquero tied the horse to a tree. Each of them took a bow, a quiver of arrows, and one blanket. They left quickly, going at right angles across the ridges.

They were only four ridges away when they heard the shout. The pursuing Arivaipa Apaches had found the horses. Running was no good now. Vaquero and Buck found a place at the head of a small canyon that offered a good fort-up behind rocks.

They did not have to wait long.

After they caught the flick of movement in several places in the trees below them, Vaquero called out in Apache. It took five minutes of negotiation before an Indian showed himself. By that time the two white men were well surrounded, but they had an overhanging cliff at their backs and a rock barrier directly in front of them.

Since it was a fairly long downhill shot, Buck kept his sights centered on the dirty breechclout of the big Apache who had stepped out from the trees to talk.

Vaquero translated. "He says he is of Hackibanzin's family, who farms in peace now on the San Pedro. He says that is where his clan is going. He thanks us for leaving the packhorse where the young men could find it easily. It was his camp that was raided by the Chiricahuas. Some of his warriors have gone on and they will soon have the Chiricahua that escaped from us. He says the raiding party was of Soldado's band."

"I knew we should have killed that Apache!" Buck growled. "Ask him about Blue and Manolito."

"I already did. He knows nothing of them."

The big Apache standing by the tree made a short speech.

"I'm going to have to learn that language. What did he say?" Buck asked.

"He wonders why, if we are friends of the Arivaipa, we hide among the rocks and will not come out and have a feast with them. They have already killed four of the Chiricahua raiders, and soon will get another one, and since they were all enemies of the White Eyes, it is strange that we will not come out of the rocks to celebrate their defeat."

"Tell him we're in too much of a hurry. We'll celebrate with them when we come down to the San Pedro later." Buck thought a moment. "And tell him that if he has his women leave four pairs of moccasins by the dead horse, I will pay him with a horse when we find him on the San Pedro."

Vaquero and the Apache talked for another three minutes.

"I told him you were the brother of John Cannon of the High Chaparral," Vaquero said. "He said that he had heard that John Cannon always spoke with a straight tongue to the Apaches, even to the Chiricahuas. He will leave the moccasins."

The Apaches disappeared as silently as they had come. Still suspecting an ambush, the two white men kept a hard watch and held their position until after sundown. Then they came out cautiously, one at a time.

"I don't know about those moccasins," Buck said. "I favor making tracks with what I got on."

"True, it is a big chance, but my feet are dying already from the little walking we have done. I am willing to take the chance."

They took a long time to go back to the dead horse. From the trees on the next ridge they studied the scene. The horse had been crudely butchered and flies were buzzing thickly around it. "There's some moccasins by it, sure enough," Buck said. "Bait, huh?"

"I don't know."

After a coyote with three big-eared whelps came out

of the trees and began to snap at the entrails, Vaquero rose and, with no more stalking, went over to the horse. The coyotes whisked away before he had taken three steps down the ridge.

There were four pairs of moccasins beside the carcass, and the Apaches had left one of the haunches.

Sitting on the ground, tugging the footwear on, Buck shook his head. "I'll be doggoned, Vaquero! Old Honest John Cannon has got us something to wear. This ought to be a lesson to both of us to always tell the truth to Apaches."

"I do," Vaquero said. "Most of the time I do." He flexed his toes in the moccasins. "If we ever see the San Pedro again, we must give the horse that we have promised."

"I'll see to it."

Vaquero picked up the haunch. "Let us find a place where our fire cannot be seen and we will eat."

Buck looked at the thick coating of dark blood and flies on the meat. "Ugh! Horsemeat."

"We will eat worse before we ever see the High Chaparral again."

The next morning they cached their rifles and all the cartridges for them. That left them with their pistols—and the bows and arrows. It was hard for Buck to part with his rifle, but he understood the wisdom of doing so: An arrow was a silent missile.

Vaquero said that he once had been fairly well skilled in the use of a bow. Buck would just have to do the best he could.

"We've left stuff all over Arizona Territory," Buck

said. "First, our saddles, then our boots, and now our rifles."

"As long as we don't leave our lives. . ." Vaquero reminded him.

10 Strong of Heart

AFTER THE RIGORS of the trail, Blue and Manolito found the canyon a great relief. Once the camp was established, even Pinera could not find tasks to keep them busy all the time. Both her husband and her son had been killed in a fight with Navajos the year before. Her arms bore many knife slashes that she had inflicted on herself while mourning the loss.

Cayatano had put the captives in her charge, and she was jealous of her authority, allowing no other woman to order them around. Blue and Manolito knew that scraping hides and gathering firewood and the other tasks that Pinera set for them were women's work, but they performed them willingly.

It occurred to Blue that all the menial chores he did were as essential to keeping an Apache camp running as the little, uninteresting jobs that Pa had talked about that morning long ago—those day-by-day things that kept the High Chaparral running.

Blue and Manolito found that they were being gradually accepted as part of the Apache routine. Even the children began to lose interest in jeering the captives.

The last of the cactus spines in Blue's foot had festered out, the rope marks on his neck and wrists had healed, and his knee no longer bothered him. Without the physical torment of thirst and injury to sustain anger against the Apaches, his attitude toward them was changing.

They were Indians. They had lived for centuries in a cruel, harsh land that had marked them. Their way of life had molded them in many ways into becoming as brutal as the land itself. To treat captives as Blue and Manolito had been treated by Kanseah was merely age-old custom with Apaches.

After Blue was able to bring himself to at least partial understanding of how Apaches thought, he lost his desire to kill Kanseah. He knew he never could be a friend of Kanseah, but at least he quit staring at the Apache and picking places in his hide where he would like to put a bullet.

There was no danger, anyway, of becoming truly friendly with Kanseah, for the latter's hatred of White Eyes was a solid, enduring part of the young Apache.

One day while grinding corn in a metate Blue asked Manolito, "Do you still want to kill Kanseah?"

Manolito shrugged. "I have not forgotten what he did, but thinking of him no longer makes me grind my teeth. Perhaps I would drag him a little behind my horse, if the chance came, and I think there will someday be that chance."

"When? Have you figured something out?"

"I have an idea that is growing, but it is too early yet to be hopeful."

Blue looked at the sheer red walls, and he thought of the guard on the trail. As long as they were down in the hole, he could not ever be very hopeful. As far as being rescued by someone from the High Chaparral—that was not a logical thought now.

If any considerable force ever seriously threatened the camp, Blue knew that both he and Manolito would be killed. Kanseah or Nonithian, or both, would see to that in a hurry.

Pinera watched the captives and took her ease. It was good to have two slaves at her command, especially when one of them spoke Apache. And the White Eyes was learning fast to understand the language, she realized.

It was strange how the two seemed to accept their life. They did not sulk or drag around in fear, as if they expected to be killed at any moment. They laughed and joked and did as she ordered. It was only when she saw them eyeing the canyon walls that their desire to escape was plain to see.

She studied Manolito most of all. He had the marks of a warrior. In spite of his smiling and his jokes, he was strong and tough. It was not unusual for Mexicans to live among the Apaches and become one of them. There were many like that in different bands that Pinera had seen.

Most of them, of course, had been captured when young, like Nacori. He was half Apache, but he would have grown up as a Mexican if he had not been taken in that raid seven years before in Sonora. Now he was a true Apache.

Manolito was not mourning the change in his life. He had left behind no wife and family. Every day he followed the Apache custom of washing his hair in the soapy ooze that Pinera made for him by boiling bear grass and love vine. Yes, there were many things about Manolito. . . . His eyes wandered at times to Chema, but he was wise enough not to go beyond that. Chema was going to marry Kanseah.

It was possible that Manolito would make a good husband, Pinera thought. Of course, he would remember that she had kicked him a few times and he would repay that with a beating now and then when he was angry, but that was nothing.

Suddenly he caught her eyes on him. He grinned and said, "Now what are you thinking, my pretty one?"

Pinera had not been confused by any man for a long time, but now she lowered her eyes. Then she rose quickly and found it necessary to adjust the blanket on the wickiup, and after a time she was able to scowl at Manolito and tell him to go bring water quickly.

"I think the old gal sort of likes you, Mano," Blue said.

"Be careful what you think. Women are always giving me much trouble, and this time it is not possible to ride away quickly."

Near the end of their second week in the canyon, Manolito went to Cayatano with a request. "Why is it we cannot hunt with the others? If your sister had men to hunt for her, she would no longer have to depend on those not of her family to bring her meat."

Cayatano considered the question for a long time.

"One of you can go each day," he said. He did not add that if the captive who was hunting did not return, something would happen to his friend. There was no need to say it; Manolito and the chief understood each other very well.

"The hunters go far," Cayatano said. "You will learn much about the country." He smiled. "And when you think you have learned enough to run away from us, that will be about the time I will take the camp to another distant place."

Manolito grinned. "Cayatano is wise, but have his captives shown that they are anxious to run away? Perhaps they find much of interest among his people."

"It is true. It is good. In time such things will help to bring understanding." Cayatano shook his head. "But you and the son of John Cannon can never be Apaches. Stay with us until it is time to go, and then you will be free to return to your people."

Manolito wanted to ask when the time to go would be, but he thought he had gained enough for the time being. At least he and Blue could now take turns at leaving the canyon.

After several trips up and down the trail, Blue lost his fear of it. He even learned to come down in the dark, carrying a deer on his back. The hunters were quite generous in one respect: They always let him carry the game.

Usually he hunted with Kanseah and Itsee, who was the only skinny-legged Apache Blue had ever seen. He was also somewhat of a clown. As Cayatano had said, the hunters ranged far, using only bows and arrows. The first time Blue went out, Kanseah and Itsee tried to run the legs off him.

They very nearly succeeded. But with the same determination that had kept him going when he was being led with a rope around his neck, Blue stayed with the hunters. The tireless Itsee led them up and down rough hills as if he were running for his life. Red-faced and panting, his legs on fire, Blue kept them in sight. Each time he caught up where they had stopped to rest, they took off immediately.

Sometimes Itsee set little ambushes. As Blue came staggering past, Itsee would leap out from concealment with a yelp, trying to scare the breechclout off the White Eyes.

After a dozen hunting expeditions, Blue found himself honed down to a fine physical edge. His wind was good. His legs stopped burning as if they were on fire, and he learned to trot along with the tireless Apache swing. Except for his eyes and his hair, bleached even lighter by the sun, he was as dark as an Apache.

Above his breechclout, he wore a scrap of shirt Pinera had given him. All that was left of his white man's attire was his belt. On that he had a knife in a deerhide case. Kanseah had given him the weapon. It had a broken point and some big nicks in the blade. He had managed to sharpen what was left of the edge by working it on a piece of fine sandstone.

With a quiver slung on his shoulder and a bow in his hand, Blue went out every other day with the hunters. Kanseah assumed that anyone should be able to use a bow; he had only contempt for Blue's clumsiness with the weapon. Itsee gave Blue a few lessons. It did not take Blue long to realize that he would have to shoot a few thousand arrows before he ever approached Apache efficiency with a bow.

But at fifty yards he became reasonably sure of his aim. The first deer he killed was not the one he was shooting at, but one that was standing ten feet farther up the slope. He got it through the throat by sheer accident. It ran some distance before it fell, and by that time Blue had covered up his astonishment.

Itsee saw the truth of things. He rolled on the ground and laughed until Blue had to admit his luck with a sheepish grin.

Each night in the canyon camp, the captives discussed the country around them, exchanging observations of what they had seen. And thus it was that Blue and Manolito stored up a great deal of information about the land south of where they were. That, of course, was the direction they would have to go if they ever got a chance to escape.

One night around the fire, Manolito said, "Each time you go out, I get a little nervous. Suppose you became lost and wandered away and did not return that night." He rolled his eyes and ran his hand across his throat.

"Nobody gets lost with Kanseah and Itsee, and you know I'm not going to run away."

"I was joking, *amigo*." Manolito looked at the sky. "There is a way out of this canyon at the upper end. I have studied the rocks and there is a way for one on foot. Does this suggest an idea?"

It did indeed, Blue thought. If they both could get

away at the same time, they were in condition to go through the hills, at least for a few days, almost as fast as the Apaches. Though they were not sure of the distance because they had made several detours on the way to the canyon, they thought that two days of hard travel would put them close to Sandy Lake.

"Let us not be hasty," Manolito murmured. "I must study the rocks some more." He glanced toward Chema. "And it is not too unpleasant here. Pinera does not kick me as much as she used to."

"You keep away from Chema!" Blue said. "I've seen her looking at you, but you keep away."

"That is excellent advice, *compadre,* and if I hadn't already thought of it myself, I would be grateful to you."

Blue stared at Manolito across the fire. Like Blue, he was now dressed in Apache manner. His dark hair was growing long. It would be only a question of time before he needed a headband. Except for his beard, he could almost pass as an Apache. He had even done something about that. From Pinera, whose bag of loot contained many unusual items, he had obtained a small pair of scissors with which he kept his beard trimmed as close as possible.

It seemed, in fact, that Manolito *wanted* to look like an Apache.

Blue, on the other hand, knew he simply couldn't make the grade. Every time he looked at his reflection in one of the quiet pools farther up the canyon, his bushy blond hair gave him a very un-Indian-like appearance.

Nacori came silently from the shadows behind them.

He squatted by the tiny fire and began to speak in halting English.

"Speak Apache," Blue said. He had picked up some of the language by necessity, and he felt that it might be a good idea to become as fluent in the tongue as Manolito.

Nacori gave him a startled look. He started to talk in Spanish.

"No!" Blue insisted. "Apache."

There was a lot that Blue didn't catch, but he did get the general idea of the subject matter. Nacori was asking Manolito something about soldiers, and about going home.

"Did you get it?" Manolito asked.

"Not all of it."

"He wants to know if we have changed our minds about him. If we are freed, will we still tell the soldiers about him."

"I don't think I would," Blue said. "He seems happy enough here. All his folks are gone, except—who was it?— his uncle?"

"The brother of his grandfather."

"That's not very close. He thinks more of Cayatano now than he ever would of a distant relative. What's your idea?"

"I would say nothing." Manolito looked at Nacori and made the statement in Apache. Then Blue repeated it.

Nacori said nothing. He rose and walked away.

Back in the shadows Cayatano had been listening. It was he who had sent Nacori to ask the question. Now there was an answer and it was good. As he had hoped, the two captives had changed their minds about Nacori.

But the time had not yet arrived for the final decision. Though Blue and Manolito had spoken with straight tongues, it would be wise to keep them for a longer time so that they could see more of Nacori's position in the clan, so that they would know without any doubt at all that his place was with Cayatano's people.

And it would be well for Blue and Manolito to learn more about the Apaches. No harm would come to them, unless they brought it on themselves. The more they learned about Apaches, the better the chances were that when they returned to their own people they would speak against some of the wrong ideas that the White Eyes had of Apaches.

Cayatano knew that he was seeing very far and that many Apache leaders scoffed at him and called him an old woman whose courage to fight was gone. They said that because he had lived among White Eyes miners as a boy, he was now trying in his old age to become a White Eyes himself.

Still, there were strong men among the Apaches who knew this was a lie. They listened to Cayatano when he told them that it would never be possible to love all the Pinda-lick-o-yi because their ways were too strange, but it would be possible to be friends with a few of them. The Gray Fox was one and John Cannon was another.

Since there were these two, there must be others, too, who could understand the Apaches. In time there could be peace between the two peoples, and that was all Cayatano wanted, not because he was old and afraid to fight—only the first was true—but because he knew deep in his heart that the Apaches could never win by warring against the ever-increasing numbers of Pinda-lick-o-yi.

He would do what he could while he lived, and afterward the task would be Nacori's.

Drawing his blanket tighter around him to ward off the chill of night, he watched the fire-lit faces of the two captives. They had done well, those two; they were strong of heart.

It was decided: No longer would they be slaves.

11 Flight

ON THEIR HUNTING TRIP that day Kanseah and Itsee led
Blue farther from the canyon than they had ever gone
before. For mile on mile they continued southward,
covering distance rather than hunting. Blue suspected
some trickery even before the others stopped to point
out a hill at least four miles away.

With words and gestures Kanseah explained that they
would split up, he and Itsee going off to the side, right
and left, while Blue was to go on to the pointed hill,
where the three of them would meet.

They must think I'm stupid, Blue told himself. He
tried to show no expression as he nodded.

Kanseah trotted into the thickets on the left. Itsee
went the other way, into broken country on the right.

Blue was not sure but he thought the distant hill was
part of the main divide between the desert and the
mountains. From there, he guessed, he could look far
out toward home. By trotting most of the day and into
the night, he probably could reach Sandy Lake.

He did go far enough toward the hill to set a pattern,

133

for he was sure he was being watched. And then he dropped into a brushy gully and went back toward the canyon as fast as he could. He was only about a mile from the head of the steep trail when he saw a buck browsing in the cedars.

Using every trick Kanseah and Itsee had taught him, he made his stalk, moving when the deer was eating, lying as motionless as a stone when its head was up. His arrow was true. He put it through the deer's lungs. Five minutes later he had trailed the animal down to where it fell.

When he cut its throat he had a sudden impulse to give the Apaches something to talk about. He dipped his hands in the blood and smeared it through his hair until he was no longer a sun-bleached blond.

With the deer on his shoulders he set off at a trot. From the rocks above the trail he gave the owl hoot signal to the unseen guard. It was Johze in the niche in the canyon wall. He snapped an arrow to the bowstring when he first saw Blue, and then he stared in wonder at the hunter's stiff, rust-brown hair.

Blue gave him a grin and hurried past.

The children trotted after Blue with awed expressions when he reached camp. The flies were thick around his head by then and he was having some misgivings about his little stunt. He kept a straight face as he went on to Pinera's wickiup and put the deer down. With an imperious sweep of his hand he indicated Manolito, who was loafing in the shade.

"Take care of the meat."

Staring at Blue, Pinera put her hand over her mouth.

"Have your slave take care of the meat," Blue said. He could barely keep from laughing at Manolito's expression.

Pinera touched Blue's hair hesitantly with her fingers. She rubbed the crusted residue with her thumb. "Bloody head." The wide-eyed children standing around the wickiup repeated the words.

And that was the Apache name by which Billy Blue Cannon was known ever after. Bloody Head.

Pinera waved Manolito aside. She took care of the deer herself.

The flies were something fierce around Blue, buzzing in his ears and tangling in his hair, but he continued to play it out. Then his scalp began to itch. He strutted away to the creek to wash his head. The children chattered more easily when they saw his blond hair appearing once more. But they had been impressed by what he had done.

He explained to Manolito the trick he was sure Kanseah and Itsee had tried to pull. "They figured the minute I got to the top of that hill, thinking they were both far away, that I would make a run for it."

Manolito nodded. "Ah, yes! The *ley de fuga*. Let the man escape so you can kill him. They went far beyond that hill, waiting."

"I'm sure they did. And I hope they wait there till it snows!"

It was after dark before Kanseah and Itsee returned. On top of their chagrin over being outguessed by Blue, they had to take the jeers of clan members because they had returned late with no game, while a White Eyes hunter had come back early with a fine buck.

But Kanseah had something far more serious than the failure of a trick to report to his father. He and Itsee had met two Chiricahua scouts from Soldado's band. The scouts had inquired about the captives. Weeks before, Little Calf, the nephew of Soldado, had been fleeing from angry Arivaipas when he was ambushed by two men from the High Chaparral.

Little Calf had seen them both before. They had inquired about the captives. They were seeking them and they had not been far from the secret trail at the time. Little Calf knew nothing of any captives recently taken. After he escaped from the two men of the High Chaparral and also from the pursuing Arivaipas, he returned to Soldado's camp and reported on his adventures.

And now Soldado was on the move with his band. He had sent scouts ahead to find out who had valuable captives and where they were.

Nonithian, as usual, had edged in to hear what was being reported. Now he nodded wisely. It was just as he had predicted: The captives would be nothing but trouble.

"I told the scouts that we knew nothing of a White Eyes and a Mexican from the High Chaparral," Kanseah said. "They asked then why it was that two of their companions were seeking them. I grew angry and told them that I did not know that, either."

"Yes, you grew angry," Cayatano said. That had given the scouts a very good hint at the truth, he realized. "How far away is Soldado's camp?"

"Two days, if the scouts told the truth."

No one had told much truth at that encounter, Cayatano thought, but it mattered little now. If Soldado's scouts did not already know this canyon, they would find it. He wondered what had happened to the two men of the High Chaparral who had been seeking Blue and Manolito.

"I knew we should have killed them long ago," Nonithian said. "I had a dream about them when Kanseah first brought them into camp, and today I saw strange things in the waters of a pool." He was off again with a long-tailed recital of the evil the captives were going to bring upon the clan.

When he had finished, Cayatano said curtly, "It is well that we did not kill them. Their friends know that they did not die in the flood. If we had killed them, there would be soldiers on our trail now."

"I am not afraid of soldiers," Kanseah said. "I have fought them."

Nonithian slapped his hand against the scar on his chest. "And I have fought them many times!"

Cayatano concealed his disgust. He looked calmly at the group of warriors before his wickiup. All of them together had not fought the soldiers, Mexican and White Eyes, as many times as he had. "I have no time to show my scars. We must leave this place and take the captives with us."

"Give them to Soldado," Kanseah suggested. "Then we will be free of them and he can do with them as he wishes. Let the soldiers chase him."

That was the great weakness of Apaches, Cayatano thought bitterly; they were always willing to betray each other. Even his own son could see no wrong in it. Not that Cayatano had any love for Soldado, but they were all Apaches, and the Pinda-lick-o-yi seldom knew one group from another.

If the Jicarillas killed a miner, or the Mimbrenos took a White Eyes captive, or the Coyoteros stole all the horses from a ranch, the soldiers were quick to take revenge on any Apaches they could find—Chiricahuas, Arivaipas, Mescaleros, or any band they came across. They had even been known to kill Pimas by mistake, which, of course, was not too bad.

"If harm comes to the captives, it will not matter who did it," Cayatano said. "All Apaches will be guilty. No, we will not give them to Soldado."

Nonithian said, "Since Cayatano's heart is so big for the Pinda-lick-o-yi, let us drive the captives from the canyon and let them go where they wish."

"Straight into the hands of Soldado? His scouts are probably sniffing close to the canyon even now. No," Cayatano said in disgust. "We will leave this place and take them with us to keep them from being harmed by others." Perhaps Soldado was coming from the south, and perhaps his scouts had lied, but Cayatano could take no chances.

Nonithian and Kanseah were very much against running away, and there were others, too, who saw no good reason for leaving the canyon just because of two troublesome captives.

Still, Cayatano was the leader. He had been a great fighter and he was wise. They respected him. He stood before them with his wrinkled, grim face showing no doubt at all that his decision would be accepted.

"And we will say nothing about the two White Eyes who search for them," Cayatano said. By now those two must have become discouraged and gone home, he thought; surely they had realized how foolish it was for two men to come far into Apache land.

It was not the best thing to move a whole camp in the dark hours sacred to the ancestral dead, but the Wormwood clan prepared to go. First, the scouts went up the trail and ranged out in an effort to determine whether or not Soldado's men were already watching the canyon.

They found no sign of the enemy advance party, and so the people went up the narrow trail, leading ponies along ribbon ledges across sheer walls where a slip meant a fall of hundreds of feet into eternal darkness.

No child whimpered or cried out during the ascent, no woman complained about the danger, and no one carelessly betrayed the move by knocking rocks into the depths below. Manolito and Blue were near the end of the procession. When they reached the top, those who had preceded them had already scattered by pre-arranged plan.

Only Cayatano and Nacori were waiting in the shadows of a great rock.

"Go with Nacori," the chief told Manolito and Blue.

"Where are we going?" Manolito asked.

"My son will take you there."

Blue and Manolito followed Nacori.

Trotting through the night, Blue murmured, "It would be easy to get away, Mano."

"Yes. I have been thinking that. I also think we had better trust Cayatano. There is some important reason for the camp moving so suddenly."

Sometime later Nacori told them why they were running in the night.

"Soldado?" Blue said. "We could have fought him. Mano and I would have helped."

"My father says that is what is wrong. There is too much fighting already among the Apaches. When the snows come and the bands move down from the mountains, he will get them together again and speak of this matter in a great council."

"And then go to war with the White Eyes?" Manolito asked.

"No! When the Apaches are all strong among themselves, it will be easier to make peace with the White Eyes, my father says."

"Do you believe it?"

"Yes!" Nacori said. "It will happen."

At dawn they came to the great canyon. In the early light, with shadows still in the depths below, the view was awesome. With no great love of height, Blue found himself looking for some broad, easy way to descend.

The agile Nacori took them down a route that made Blue sweat with fear. Once, clinging to the wall, Manolito glanced down and then looked up at Blue and made a face with his eyes crossed and his mouth hanging. Blue would laugh about it later, but at the moment he was too scared.

They crossed a strong-flowing river at the bottom, stopping only to drink and slop water on their faces.

"Are we still in Arizona Territory?" Blue asked.

Manolito lifted his dripping face and grinned. He looked at the mighty hills where Nacori was pointing. "The way he goes, we'll be out of the United States before long."

12 Cavalrymen

BUCK CANNON and Vaquero were about three weeks behind on the trail, and now they had no trail at all and were going toward the great canyon of the Salt River on the chance of finding there the right Apache camp. They didn't know they had missed a red-hot trail by only half an hour.

They went far enough to see part way into the deep side canyon. It was just another big hole like the many they had looked into, all of them rock-strewn, desolate places. From what they saw of this one, it was no different from the others, and so they turned away from it to seek a passable route.

By a half hour they missed seeing Blue and Kanseah and Itsee pop up from a place where it seemed no human being could, or would care to, climb either up or down.

Late that day Buck and Vaquero found an easy descent into the great main canyon. Looking at the walls across the rushing stream, and then glancing back at the way they had come down, Buck said, "I can see now why Apaches move on foot better than they do on

142

horses. An animal couldn't do it."

Vaquero was sure that somewhere along the river they would find a rancheria. It was possible sometimes to walk right into an Apache camp and walk out again. That depended on what band it was. If they found a rancheria, they would scout it out first to determine whether or not Blue and Manolito were there. After that. . . . As Buck had said, they would have to think of what to do then.

And now Vaquero's statement that they had to live like Indians came into full significance. Every rock and every turn had to be approached cautiously. They had to be like wild animals, wary every minute of their waking hours, sleeping by turns at night. They subsisted on what they could kill with arrows. Sometimes the fare was lean. They did not quite get down to rats, but Buck had decided that it was possible.

Whenever they could they retrieved their arrows, but they broke or lost many of them. They had only a few good points left the day, far downstream from the big canyon, when they found the rancheria.

It was deserted.

There were corn and squash and melon patches in the sandy loam beside the river, but nothing was matured. From the articles scattered around the camp, it appeared that the Apaches had left in haste not long before.

Vaquero studied the signs carefully. "Soldiers. Scouts saw them before they were close, and the camp picked up and moved."

They found nothing to prove that Blue and Manolito had been at the rancheria. Beside a wickiup Buck found arrow shafts and points that someone had forgotten during the hasty flight. He gathered them up, while Vaquero took a small *tus,* a pitch-smeared water jar.

It took only a little scouting to show that the Apaches had scattered in all directions. Vaquero shook his head. "Until we have some knowledge of where to go. . . ." He spread his hands to show the futility of searching blindly for the captives.

"If we hang out in the canyon, sooner or later we'll catch one or two Indians by themselves," Buck said. "We'll get ourselves a prisoner who can tell us something."

"If we happen to get a man who knows anything about Blue and Manolito."

"The moccasin telegraph works pretty good," Buck said. "There's a chance that a lot of Apaches know about Blue and Mano."

Vaquero nodded. "Yes, there is that chance."

All the time that Blue and Manolito were with Cayatano's clan in the secret canyon, sometimes not more than three miles from the searchers, Buck and Vaquero ranged the gigantic slash in the earth, waiting for their chance to grab an Apache.

They saw the tracks of ponies and of Indians on foot, and of small parties that had crossed the canyon at various times, but Buck and Vaquero were never in the right place at the right time to intercept. Twice they went back to the rancheria site to see if it had been reoccupied, but it was still abandoned.

One evening while they were staying in a cave across the river from a grassy spot, a party of ten Indians came off the high hills, driving a herd of ponies, and camped beside the stream.

Lying in the darkness of their cave, Vaquero and Buck watched them. There were no women and children in the bunch. It was a raiding party which had stolen the ponies somewhere up north. From the looks of the herd, they had been driven at a killing pace.

The Apaches butchered one of the ponies for supper. The watchers in the cave saw them roasting guts and chunks of meat around their small fires.

"Do you reckon we could sneak in tonight and grab ourselves a sentry?" Buck asked.

"If we capture one, we'll have to capture ten. No, *amigo,* we must wait for a better chance."

Soon after daylight the raiders went downriver with their stolen ponies. They abandoned one limping animal. Just before leaping on his mount, an Apache stooped and with a quick slash cut the tendon on the hind leg of the hobbling pony.

"The dirty—" Buck choked down his outrage.

"They expect to be pursued, and so they leave nothing for the owners of the herd, but they have left meat for us."

They went across the river and killed the crippled pony and butchered it. "See those sores on its back and shoulders?" Vaquero said. "That is the part Apaches eat first because it is the most tender."

They barely made it across the river and into the rocks with their meat before the pursuers showed up. Fifteen more Apaches, who spent little time at the campsite before racing down the river.

"If they're not killing us, they're killing each other," Vaquero said. "It is like Mexico."

They went upriver to a hiding place where they could smoke the meat into jerky.

Four days later they were close to a good campsite several miles down the river. They waited there all day in the hopes of catching one or two Apaches by themselves. Now it was late and it did not seem that anyone was going to use the campsite that night.

Buck decided to take a bath. Vaquero was standing guard in a niche in the rocks from which he could overlook the underbrush. With his head just above water, Buck rubbed his whiskered face. "Another week or two of this and I'll be the old man of the mountains. Maybe we're making a big mistake staying here, when all the time—"

Vaquero signaled for silence.

Buck scrambled out of the pool and grabbed his pistol.

Though the noise of the river and the intervening growth made the sounds indistinct, they were loud enough to tell that visitors were down at the campsite.

Buck dressed as fast as he could. At the last moment he remembered to take his bow and arrows before he and Vaquero slipped into the brush and began their wary stalk.

They came to a turn in the canyon. The noises were louder then. Buck motioned for his companion to stay where he was, while he crawled on ahead to where the brush thinned out.

Suddenly Buck rose with a disgusted grunt. He put

his pistol away and called for Vaquero to come.

The grassy spot beside the river about a hundred yards away was filled with cavalrymen. When Buck called to Vaquero some of the soldiers leaped for their carbines.

"Hold it, you knotheads!" Buck yelled. He held both hands high, waving his hat. In spite of his shout and waving arms, three of the soldiers took hasty shots at the strange-looking figure that had popped out of the willows so suddenly. The heavy bullets whipped into the brush close to Buck. Vaquero had just risen. He dived flat on his belly again.

A tall sergeant bellowed at the nervous cavalrymen, and there was no more shooting.

Lt. Kingsley Bruton was in charge of the scouting party of twenty men. The first question he asked was, "What in blazes are you two doing out here in those Apache moccasins?"

Buck scratched his whiskers. "Well, Lieutenant, we've found these here moccasins right comfortable," he drawled. "You knew General Crook issued an order the other day that all his mule infantry had to wear moccasins from now on."

The lieutenant was not as stuffy as Buck had thought. He grinned. "Not a bad idea. I've tried them myself."

"Looking for some horses the Apaches got," Buck said blandly. "Five head run off from Sandy Lake by Chiricahuas." The last thing he wanted was the Army taking charge of the job he and Vaquero had set out to do. If soldiers took a crack at an Apache camp where captives were, the first to die would be the captives.

Lieutenant Bruton eyed Buck and Vaquero shrewdly.

"Five horses, eh? They must have been valuable animals."

"Oh, they were!" Buck said.

The tall sergeant had a half-grin on his grizzled features. "Begging your pardon, Lieutenant, I think this man is Big John Cannon's brother from the High Chaparral. Buck, ain't it? I seem to remember having a little discussion with him in a cantina one night in Tucson."

"That you did!" Buck laughed. "I think my ribs are still sore from that little discussion."

Bruton cleared his throat. "Post the sentries, Sergeant." He looked at Buck. "Five horses, eh? Where's your mounts, Cannon?"

Buck grinned. "We donated them to an Apache one night."

The soldiers were caring for their horses, building cooking fires, preparing to camp. A wrinkled little man with a big Sharps rifle came over to listen to the discussion. Soon he and Vaquero had moved aside and were talking in quick-flowing Spanish.

"Well, Cannon, we haven't seen anything of your— ah—five valuable horses," Lieutenant Bruton said.

Buck grinned. "You don't seem to believe me."

"Let's say I'm rather startled to find two lone men this deep in dangerous country, chasing after Apaches with five horses. Now, if you had made it twenty animals and there were ten of you. . . . Of course, it's your business."

"Sure now," Buck drawled. "How's the Apache sign been where you were?"

"Plenty! Smoke on the hills, mirror signals, campsites with big mescal pits, pony tracks." Bruton shook his head. "We scouted fifty miles north of here and made one contact—three scared squaws and a buck from old Cayatano's bunch. That was yesterday."

"No loose horses, huh?"

"Three scroungy ponies. The buck had a fair-looking sorrel. My guide said—" Bruton looked at the man talking to Vaquero. "Peeples, what was it you said about that sorrel the sullen young buck was riding yesterday?"

The guide was leaning on his rifle. He spat tobacco juice. "Kanseah? Old Cayatano's son? Looked like the shoes on that sorrel had been jerked not too long back. Apache saddle on him, but you could see where he was just starting to hair out again from the wear of a regular saddle with a breast strap. Blaze like a lance point. White stockings except for the left rear leg."

Manolito's horse!

Buck glanced at Vaquero. "That don't quite fit none of the five we lost, does it?"

Vaquero shook his head.

"Stolen mount, of course," Lieutenant Bruton said. "The rider said he had traded for the horse in Sonora." He shrugged. "I assume you'll return with us as far as Sandy Lake?"

"We'll think on it," Buck said. "It's a fact we don't seem to be getting anywhere." So Cayatano had Blue and Mano! Why, heck, he was the one that Big John always thought was halfway friendly.

Buck and Vaquero ate with Sergeant McBride, Buck's onetime adversary in a Tucson brawl, and Tom Peeples, the leathery little guide. The scouting detail was on Spartan rations, hardtack with weevils in it, coffee, and

rancid bacon. Some of them had improved their fare
with game. Peeples and McBride had part of a deer left.
After horsemeat, it was a welcome change to Buck and
Vaquero, and so was the coffee Peeples made. It was
strong enough to float a cartridge.

"You ain't hunting no horses, Cannon," Peeples said
while they were sitting around the fire after eating.

"We're not?" Buck watched Sergeant McBride going
toward Bruton's tiny fire. "I'll say one thing for your
lieutenant there, Peeples; he travels light."

Peeples puffed his pipe. "Good man. A few like him
and we might get somewhere with the Apaches."

"Extermination, you mean?"

"No. He believes like old Crook hisself. Says we could
get along with the Apaches—most of them, that is—if we
half-tried to be honest. You ain't looking for horses."

"Did Vaquero tell you that?" Buck asked.

"Worse liar than you are, Cannon, but at least he
didn't give nothing away when I described that sorrel.
You did. You've got a pretty fair poker face, but I thought
you was going to crush that bow with your right fist."
Peeples took an ember from the fire and lit his pipe.

"Now, did I do that?" Buck murmured.

"Your business, of course, like the lieutenant says, but
if I was looking for someone who had a sorrel horse
that belongs to old Don Sebastian Montoya's son—"

"You didn't say any of that before." Buck glanced at
Vaquero.

"Just now hit me," Peeples said. "I knew I'd seen that
sorrel somewhere, but not until I got to thinking about
the High Chaparral did it hit me. Was that wild young

Mexican, old Don Sebastian's son—what's his name?"

"Manolito," Vaquero said.

"Yeah! Was he riding the sorrel when the Apaches—"

"Yes," Buck said. "They got two, Manolito and my nephew, Billy Blue Cannon. We lost the trail weeks ago on the south side of the canyon."

"Now, that's a pair for the Apaches to grab!" Peeples said. "There'll really be a going-up-the-mountain such as you never did see when old Montoya and Big John Cannon start bellering. Why, half the Army will be—"

"That's just what we don't want," Buck said.

Peeples nodded. "I've been in a camp or two after the Army made a well-meaning rush at Apaches with white prisoners. I remember three little— Well, never mind that." He shook his head. "But just you two alone . . . I don't know, boys."

Buck and Vaquero looked at each other quietly.

Peeples knocked the dottle from his pipe into the palm of his hand. He blew away the ashes carefully to save what was left of the tobacco. "I know what you mean about the Army, Cannon. Howsomever, this here Lieutenant Bruton is considerable different, like I said. I don't think you'd go wrong asking help from him."

Buck shook his head. "*He* may be all right, Peeples, but two or three of his soldiers took shots at me after I stepped out of the brush with this beard that a blind man should have been able to see."

"Yeah. One shot at the wrong time around an Apache camp. . . . Yeah, I know."

"Where'd you see the sorrel?" Vaquero asked.

Peeples told him the location, and then he described

three likely places where Cayatano might camp for a while.

"You're sure it was Cayatano's son on the sorrel?" Buck asked.

"Lived with that clan one summer," Peeples said curtly.

Buck stared at the ground. "Cayatano and Big John know each other. They always got along, but now he's grabbed Blue and Mano. That just goes to show you how far you can trust an Apache."

"Kanseah had the sorrel," Peeples said. "Where he got it is something else. You can't say who's got your boys."

"That's what hurts," Buck said grimly. "But there's only one way to find out if Cayatano has them."

"Yep." Peeples studied Buck keenly. "I can ask Bruton to let me go with you. Might be some help."

"To recover five stolen horses?" Buck shook his head. "He's suspicious of that story already, and now if you ask him to let you go with us, that'll give it away for sure."

"Probably. He'd most likely spin this detail around on its hindlegs and take after Cayatano." Peeples dumped the shards of tobacco from his palm into a pouch. "Maybe he'll do just that, anyway."

"Not if you don't say anything."

"He ain't dumb by no means."

"Nobody said he was. I appreciate your offer, Peeples, but I guess me and Vaquero will play it our own way."

The guide nodded. "Your business, Cannon." He dropped a handful of twigs on the fire. "Your people, too. Well, you've got all night to think about it."

"Already thought about it."

In the chill of false dawn Buck and Vaquero rose quietly and gathered up their few possessions. Lying with his heavy rifle under the blanket, Tom Peeples opened his eyes at their first movement. "Good luck," he said.

They saw no one else awake in camp. It looked like an easy strike for Apaches. And then not far beyond the grassy place they ran squarely into a sentry concealed in the rocks.

"Still set on going after them horses, huh?" he asked.

"That's a fact, bucko." Buck looked down at the sleeping camp. "How many sentries are out?"

"Six others."

None of the six were in evidence, not even near the horses.

"Lieutenant Bruton believes in keeping a tight watch on things," the sentry said.

"So it seems." A third of the detail on guard, Buck thought. Even Apaches would have a devil of a time trying to surprise one of Bruton's camps. Maybe he should have taken Peeples' advice and asked for a little help, but he could not forget that some of Bruton's men had been a mite too sudden with their trigger fingers.

One mistake like that could cost Blue and Manolito their lives.

"See you, bucko," Buck said to the sentry. He followed Vaquero up the steep hill.

They were only two days behind now. It was that close, if they were on the right trail.

13 Ransom for the Captives

THOUGH CAYATANO was too old and experienced in the ways of his people to consider any place in the mountains or desert completely safe, he was reasonably sure that the clan could rest for a while at Beyota. That was the name of the high valley where the camp was now snugged in beside a stream that tumbled down from the dense thickets of scrub oaks.

He sat beside his wickiup and watched Blue and Manolito talking to the children, the same children who had jeered the captives and beaten them with sticks not long before.

It was good. If the young of both the White Eyes and the Apaches could learn at an early age to know each other, then there would be less hatred. At the edge of the group, Nacori was standing apart, watching with a solemn look.

With three stones of different colors Manolito was showing the children a version of the ancient stick game of the Apaches. His hands were very quick. He shook the stones between his palms and then rubbed them briskly, talking all the time, and then when he held his clenched fists out, the children tried to guess where the green stone was.

They were never right; it had always disappeared. Manolito would then find it in the headband of one of the boys or in the fold of his moccasin leg.

Nacori tried not to show any interest. He was too old to take part in any such childish game, unless there was gambling for ponies, but he watched.

Nonithian, too, pretended that the performance was a silly thing not worthy of attention, but Cayatano observed how his eyes kept darting from Manolito's hands to the places where he found the green stone. Nonithian was as mystified as the children.

The medicine man limped over to Cayatano. "So this is what we risk great trouble for." He jerked his hand in a scornful gesture toward Manolito. "For slaves who do simple tricks for children."

"They are no longer slaves," Cayatano said.

"Your sister does her own work now, and she is making new moccasins for Bloody Head and the Mexican."

Medicine men were like the rocks of the mountains, Cayatano thought wearily; they were around forever. But at least the stones were silent.

"Pinera looks with favor on the Mexican," Nonithian said. "She would like to have him as her husband. I have seen this in her eyes." He struck his breast. "But I remember where I got this scar, and I know that Mexicans are our enemies forever."

"There will be no marriage between Manolito and Pinera. She knows that."

Nonithian shifted to another complaint. "As I saw in my dream, the soldiers chase us, and who knows where the scouts of Soldado are? Soon we will be running every day like hunted animals, and all because of the slaves."

"The soldiers that Kanseah saw were not chasing us," Cayatano said. "They knew nothing of Bloody Head and Manolito."

"They asked about the horse."

There was a shout of laughter from the children. Nacori edged closer to the group. Nonithian scowled.

"They did not take the horse," Cayatano said. "Yes, they will know about those two over there." But by that time, Cayatano thought, the captives would have been returned to their own people. If he had seen the soldiers, it could have been done then.

There was, of course, no way to satisfy Nonithian. "I had another dream about the slaves. . . ."

Cayatano appeared to be listening, but his mind was on Soldado's band. That was where the danger lay. Even now Kanseah and Itsee were scouting to see if any of Soldado's men had followed across the big canyon.

If Kanseah and Pinera and the two other women had not taken such a roundabout way and been so long in getting to Beyota, Cayatano would have known about the soldiers sooner. Then he could have let Bloody Head and Manolito go to them, and everything would have been good.

But now the soldiers were far away, for they had been riding back to their big camp below the Running Water. Between them now and Beyota, Soldado's scouts or others who hated the White Eyes were sure to be prowling. He knew that well.

No, Cayatano could not tell his visitors to go in freedom, for if they did not get back safely to their people,
not only the Wormwood clan, but all Apaches, would be
blamed.

Cayatano wished there were more Apaches who could
understand such facts. He wished Kanseah had never
captured the pair, in the first place. And he wished fer-
vently that Nonithian would keep still and have no more
long-tailed dreams.

There was much that the old chief did not know, or
he would have been even more worried.

Soldado's scouts were no longer two; there were now
six of them, all lean and deadly Chiricahuas. They had
crossed the big canyon and were unraveling the many
trails that Cayatano's clan had made. It would be only
a question of time before they found Cayatano's new
camp.

They had found the former camp in the secret canyon
the day after Cayatano fled from it. Then they had seen
a camp of twenty soldiers beside the Salt River. Perhaps
the striped-legs had already recovered the captives, or
at least they must have been sent to find them.

For a whole day the Chiricahuas of Soldado's band
spied on the soldiers. It was a well-guarded camp. They
saw Big Rifle, the guide. He was to be feared because he
was like an Apache himself, and he knew all the places
in the mountains.

He was the only one in camp not wearing soldier
clothing, the heavy shirts and pants that covered white

skins and made the wearers very hot. No, the soldiers had not found Cayatano's captives, but it was strange that they were merely staying by the river. Usually they were always in a hurry when they were in the mountains.

Soldado's men watched all day, and then they went around the camp in the evening and into the steep hills to find Cayatano's trail. Unless he kept running north, there were three likely places for him to stop.

Now all the signs were pointing to Beyota, where the acorns would be ripe in another month.

No one in Lieutenant Bruton's detail ever knew that six Chiricahuas had watched them all day and then bypassed their camp. The men welcomed the chance to rest. They talked eagerly about being back in Camp Grant in a few days.

The lieutenant had something on his mind, however. It was not entirely for the purpose of resting the detail that he stayed an extra day in the canyon.

He called Tom Peeples aside for a talk.

"Cannon and Vaquero—I'm a little concerned about them, Tom."

Peeples shrugged. "Have to take care of themselves, I guess."

"You had a long talk with them. They're not chasing after stolen horses, are they?"

"Said they were."

"Uh-huh." Bruton studied the guide sharply. "I know you share the common civilian opinion of the Army, Tom, but that doesn't change the fact that I have orders to go after white captives whenever I hear about them."

"Ain't heard of none, have you?"

"I think so. Did you happen to notice the way Cannon clenched his fist on that Apache bow he was holding while you were describing that sorrel horse? And how quick he was to make sure that Vaquero would say nothing to indicate that it was a High Chaparral mount?"

"Didn't much notice, I guess," Peeples said. He rummaged in his coat for a chew of tobacco. "High Chaparral horse, huh? Who says?"

"Sergeant McBride."

"Must have a good memory for horses."

"So do you, Tom. Of course, if you had never seen it before. . . ."

Peeples squinted at the bore of his rifle. "Got something in mind, Lieutenant?"

"Yep. In the morning this detail goes back the way we just came. I intend to pick up Kanseah's trail and follow it if it takes us clear to the Mogollon Rim."

"Thought so," Peeples said. "Know what happens when a passel of cavalry barrels head-on into an Indian camp where there's captives?"

"I'm depending on you to prevent us from doing just that. Who are they, Tom?"

The guide met Bruton's steady look but he did not answer.

"All right, you don't have to say. You've made a promise to Cannon, and you've kept it."

The next morning after breakfast the cavalrymen groaned and complained to each other when, instead of riding south, Lieutenant Bruton led them into the hills from which they had just come.

Three of them suffered the punishment of walking and having to lead their horses, this to remind them of the error of firing at just anything that popped out of the brush.

Sergeant McBride had no sympathy for them. "On top of being nervous Nellies," he rasped, "you didn't even hit the man. So walk and be happy."

They walked but they were not happy.

Even in the roughest country Lieutenant Bruton kept flankers out. His rear guard consisted of the three men under punishment; they were always a few hundred yards behind, struggling to keep up.

Soon after leaving the river, Peeples found signs of Soldado's scouts, all in one party. Later the tracks diverged into three groups. The cavalrymen labored on through the hills to where they had met Kanseah. Peeples was ahead. When the soldiers came up, he had read the sign.

Cannon and Vaquero had found the place, sure enough, and they had gone on following Kanseah's trail. There were also two more pairs of moccasin tracks, made the day before, probably by two of the Apaches from the group of six whose sign Peeples had seen earlier that day. He gave the lieutenant a brief summary of his observations.

"Well, what do you make of it all?" Bruton asked.

Peeples spat. "Hills are getting overpopulated." Two outfits were chasing after the captives now—the soldiers, and Buck Cannon and Vaquero. Maybe there was a third bunch, Peeples thought to himself—other Apaches.

"Do you want to hang on to the tracks, or shortcut by

guessing?" Bruton asked him.

"Considering."

"Where's a likely place for Cayatano to light?"

"Anywhere between here and Santa Fe." Peeples thought about the three likely places he had mentioned to Buck Cannon. "I'll take a guess on something a mite closer than Santa Fe."

"That's good enough for me. Let's hear it."

The guide made his guess. It happened to be the right one. Beyota.

After returning from Coral Wash, even before he went into the house to tell Victoria the bad news, Big John Cannon dispatched a rider to Sonora to inform Don Sebastian about Manolito and Blue.

For a few moments he stood looking at the buildings of the High Chaparral, and then he went to the house.

Victoria turned pale when he told her the story.

"Are you all right?" Big John asked. "I mean, do you need a drink of water or—"

"I need nothing! I am all right." Victoria sat down carefully. "You do not know that they were tumbled under the sand. You do not know that!"

"No, we don't know. If I don't hear something from Buck within a few days, I'll get some men and go back to the wash and start digging."

"You sent Vaquero with Buck to look?"

Big John leaned on the table with both hands, staring out of the window. "No, I didn't send Buck or Vaquero anywhere, but I know that as soon as I rode away, they hightailed for the wash to see what they could turn up.

We'll hear from Buck before long."

No word came from anyone at Sandy Lake during the week that followed. Nor did Don Sebastian send any message. The rider Big John had sent to Sonora did not return. That was no great worry because the man was one of the *vaqueros* Big John had hired in Tucson, and he had not been interested in staying long in Arizona Territory in the first place.

Though he did his best not to let his own worry communicate itself to others, everyone at the High Chaparral could see how deeply disturbed Big John Cannon was.

If some word would come from someone, even bad news, it would be a relief.

Then Don Sebastian rode into the High Chaparral with four *vaqueros*. Weary and coated with dust, he was still a proud, erect figure on a beautiful black horse. He dismounted stiffly, favoring one leg. He shook hands with Big John, and then Victoria came running out to embrace her father.

Speaking softly over her shoulder, Don Sebastian asked, "There is nothing yet?"

John Cannon shook his head gravely. "I'll tell you everything after you've had time to refresh yourself."

Don Sebastian was bathing in his room when the lookout on the roof yelled, "Apache!" It was difficult to tell whether he had shouted in the singular or plural, but since he had not fired his rifle, no attack was imminent.

Big John ran outside. "Where is he, Pedro?"

"In the saguaro across the wash, *señor*, and he is signaling with a white rag, I think."

"Just one Apache?"

"That is all I see."

"Tell him to come on in," Big John said.

Pedro carried on a shouted conversation with the Indian in Spanish. "No, he will not come in. He desires that you go out to him."

Big John took Pedro with him and walked across the wash. The Apache was taller than the average Indian. Unarmed except for a knife in a turquoise-studded case, he stood with folded arms and watched the white men with his lips set in a cruel, hard line.

When they were close, he kicked something toward them.

Big John stared down at a pair of dusty, worn boots lashed together with a piece of rawhide. Blue's boots!

"Where is he?" he asked. "Where is he?"

The Apache's eyes darted to the interpreter, who put the question in Spanish. The Indian answered swiftly, talking for several moments.

"He is of Cayatano's clan," Pedro said. "Your son and the son of Don Sebastian Montoya are in Cayatano's camp not far away. They must be ransomed."

Cayatano! It did not seem possible, Big John thought. Why, he and Cayatano had got along fine. "Tell him I want to visit the camp and see Cayatano."

Pedro repeated the request. The Apache shook his head. Then again he spoke rapidly for several moments, and at the end he pointed toward the hills.

"The ransom must be delivered at Sandy Lake," Pedro said, "and then the captives will be freed. For each one Cayatano wants ten rifles and a thousand rounds of ammunition."

"Before I give them an empty shell, I'd have to see Blue and Manolito. Tell him that, Pedro."

The Apache was unimpressed by the message. He pointed at the hill again.

"What does he mean by that?" Big John asked.

"By the time the last of the sun is gone from the hill, he must have your answer. If you do not agree, your son and the son of Don Sebastian will be hung over the slow fire." Pedro shook his head. "This is not a nice thing to think about. Sometimes—"

"That will do! Tell him I must have time to think about his demand." Big John glanced at the hill. He had about a half hour, he estimated. He picked up the boots and tramped away. Pedro gave the Apache the message and then he backed off slowly before turning to follow John Cannon.

Don Sebastian was pacing the living room, wearing a dressing gown over his hastily donned clothes. He and Victoria stood side by side while John Cannon repeated the conversation with the Apache.

"Ah, yes, ransom." Don Sebastian sat down slowly. "The Apaches know that ransom is something we can understand."

"I still can't believe that Cayatano would do it," Big John said. "I just can't believe it!"

"Believe the very worst about Apaches and it will be true," Don Sebastian said. "I have fought them for more than half a century." He smoothed his thin white hair. "You say you asked to go to the camp?"

"I did and he refused."

Don Sebastian took a deep breath. He glanced at his

daughter. "Ten thousand rifles could not bring them back now."

"You think they're dead?" Big John asked.

Don Sebastian nodded.

Big John hit the table with his clenched hand. "I won't accept that! Here we've just found out that they didn't drown in Coral Wash"— he pointed at the boots on the table—"and you're saying they're dead."

"I do not know this Cayatano for whom you have such high regard, but I have heard of him. Many years ago he raided in Sonora. It was his band that killed everyone but three children at the rancho of my dear friend Sanchez Navarro.

"No, I do not know him, but he is an Apache. He asks for ransom but he will not let you see the prisoners." Don Sebastian touched his heart. "Here, I wish to believe." He touched his head. "But here, I know he lies. How long has it been?"

"Over a month now," Victoria said.

"And this is the first word they have sent." Don Sebastian shook his head slowly. "They have nothing to give us for twenty rifles. Nothing."

Big John stared through the window at the hill where the sun would soon be gone. It was the same hill on which he last had seen Blue.

"Twenty rifles," Don Sebastian said. "Two thousand cartridges. How many men, women, and children will die here, in Sonora, on the roads, at lonely ranchos, in the hills—everywhere—if we give rifles to your friend Cayatano?"

"The traders supply them, anyway!"

"Would you give them more?"

Big John scowled. "I hope to get it switched around to horses and cows in the final bargaining."

Don Sebastian rose with effort, lurching a little. "My knees have grown old," he apologized. "Give them nothing."

"That Apache might be telling the truth," Big John insisted. "I can't understand why it took so long for them to come here. I don't understand Cayatano's part in this, either. All I know is maybe the Apache is telling the truth. We can't throw away what little chance there is."

Don Sebastian had started toward the stairway. He stopped, staring straight ahead, and then he turned to look at Big John. "If you can get their demand for rifles changed to horses, I will supply the horses. I will do this to keep alive the little chance you speak of." He paused. "But only if they agree to let us see our sons before the exchange."

Victoria started to take his arm to help him up the steps. He shook his head and waved her away.

Big John strode outside. "Pedro!"

Again they went out across the wash. The Apache was not where they had seen him before. As they stood there waiting, he appeared behind them. Pedro swung around with a startled grunt. "We should kill him, I think!"

"Tell him what I told you."

The Apache did not like it. His face grew dark as Pedro spoke of ransom in terms of ponies instead of rifles. When Pedro came to the part about Big John's insisting on seeing the captives prior to paying ransom, the Indian shook his head violently.

Suddenly he broke off the negotiations. He turned on his heel and trotted off into the paloverde, and a few moments later they heard his pony racing away.

"I think there is something strange here," Pedro said. "If he has your son and the son of Don Sebastian, why did he run away so soon? Why did he not bargain?" Pedro moved his hands up and down, as if balancing weights. "Ten ponies, five rifles . . . one rifle, fifteen ponies . . . why did he not do this, instead of growing angry and running away?"

That was a question that was troubling Big John.

The only evidence he had that Blue and Manolito were alive was a pair of worn-out boots. How good was the word of the Apache who had just left so suddenly?

"If they are alive now, the Apaches will keep them alive in order to get the guns or the ponies—or whatever you pay," Pedro said. "But. . . ." He let the thought die.

Big John glared at Pedro. Another one who had given Blue and Manolito up for dead. No matter if things did point that way, John Cannon was not going to quit as long as there was the least hope left.

If he could just talk to Cayatano himself.

John Cannon decided to return to Sandy Lake. Cayatano was in the habit of camping in that area in the summer. The messenger had talked about delivering the ransom at Sandy Lake, which was further evidence to indicate that Cayatano was somewhere close to the lake.

If Don Sebastian felt able to tackle the trip, let him come along, too.

14 "A Terrible Mess"

BLUE AND MANOLITO were enjoying life at Beyota. Pinera cooked for them. They were free to do as they pleased, though when they went hunting, they were sure that Itsee and Kanseah, or some of the other men, were never very far away, keeping an eye on them.

It was not Cayatano's men who were barring their escape now, but the fear that Soldado's scouts were in the vicinity.

"We know that Soldado's men were searching for you," Cayatano said. "I do not believe they have given up. We will know better what to do when our own scouts are sure whether or not Soldado is coming with a large party. If that is so, then we will have to run again. If it is not true, then we will return to Sandy Lake."

"Maybe we could slip past Soldado's scouts by ourselves," Manolito suggested.

"You are not good enough Apaches for that." Cayatano smiled. "But you are learning quickly. I know you can no longer stay with us, so I have only one thought for you now."

"And what is that?" Manolito asked.

"To return you safely to your people, so that no Apaches will be blamed for your deaths. You have promised to say nothing of Nacori."

Manolito nodded. "The promise will be kept. Now, when will we be returned?"

"I will let you know when the time comes." The truth of the matter was that Cayatano was greatly worried. The clan knew that Soldado's men were seeking them. As long as Bloody Head and Manolito were in the camp, no one could feel secure.

While there had been no threats lately against their lives, Bloody Head and Manolito were living on a thin edge. If misfortune struck the camp, Apache tempers would flare and Nonithian would convince the clan that it was all because of the captives. The only one who would stand with Cayatano would be Nacori.

Kanseah, who had started the whole thing, would be able to think only as a warrior.

Though it appeared that Cayatano had no plan at all, and was merely waiting for Providence to solve his problem, that idea was far from the truth. He was waiting with Apache patience for his scouts to determine the strength of Soldado's advance force, and where Soldado himself was.

When those facts were known, Cayatano's clan would scatter again, leaving many trails to the north. Bloody Head and Manolito would go south, with Nacori and Itsee guiding them. Once they got around Soldado's band, they should have no trouble going all the way to Sandy Lake. Cayatano would have kept his promise, and no blood would have been spilled to make the White Eyes shout angrily for revenge against all Apaches.

And the Wormwood clan of Chiricahuas would be happy again, without strangers in their midst to make them uneasy. Of course, Nonithian would find something bad to dream about, but that was to be expected.

Cayatano sat so long in silence that Blue and Manolito knew the talk was finished. Manolito went to the wickiup to take a nap. Blue wandered upstream to a waterfall.

Squatting in the bushes, he watched fat trout feeding in the shallow fan of the pool below the waterfall. He picked insects from the bushes and flipped them off his thumbnail. When they drifted close to the big fish, the trout broke water just enough to suck them in.

Blue put an arrow to the bowstring. His first shot missed and the trout streaked into the deep water upstream. After a time one of them ventured out again, rising to the insects Blue flipped into the stream. The next time he shot, he allowed for the deflecting nature of the water.

He had learned something of patience in his weeks with the Apaches. In three hours' time he had four large trout, cleaned and strung on a willow.

Blue took them back proudly to Pinera.

After one horrified look at the fish, she ordered him to throw them away.

"No! I'm going to eat them."

Pinera snatched the willow from his hand and hurled the trout into the oak brush.

Blue was outraged, but before he could say anything, someone put a hand on his shoulder and he turned to see Cayatano standing behind him.

"Unclean," the chief said. "Long ago fish caused the great sickness among the people. Game was scarce. The people ate fish. The spots from the fish broke out on their bodies and brought a fever and many of the people died."

What a silly superstition, Blue thought. Apaches ate spoiled meat and rats and other things and never even got a bellyache, but the thought of fresh fish was enough to scare the daylights out of them. He knew better than to argue.

"Now I have learned," he said. He went up the hill and dug a hole with a stick and buried the trout.

Manolito got in on the last part of it and was highly amused. "Any good Apache knows about fish," he jibed.

"I'm not a good Apache and I'm not planning to be one!"

Manolito laughed. "Let us go find better game, *amigo*."

They hunted not only for game but also for the purpose of learning all they could about the country. Though they were sure that Cayatano would keep his word about freeing them, they thought a working knowledge of the terrain might prove very useful in case of emergency.

They went a long distance south across the hills. Mindful of the fact that Cayatano was worried about scouts from Soldado's band, they moved warily. It seemed that no one from the camp was keeping an eye on them, though that was something they could never be sure about.

In the trees they stayed about a hundred feet apart.

When they traveled parallel ridges, however, they were often much greater distances apart, and then they used simple Apache hand signals to communicate with each other.

They were on separate ridges when they came to a broken area where all the drainage suddenly dipped southward. If they went much farther, they would be descending steep hills and leaving the thickets that lay between the ridges.

Manolito signaled, *Let's go back.*

Blue gave the sign, *Let's look.*

They both were close to the end of the ridges when Blue stopped suddenly. He had caught the odor of wood smoke. Manolito apparently had not smelled it, for he kept moving until he saw Blue's danger signal.

And now they were both like Apaches on the prowl, showing themselves only briefly as they crept ahead. The smoke was coming up from somewhere beyond the end of the ridges. Though Blue could still smell it, he saw none rising in the air.

All he could think of was that it must be smoke from the fire of some of Soldado's scouts who had grown un- usually careless. Even if they were such bunglers, they were about the last people in all the world that he cared to encounter.

Looking across at Manolito occasionally, Blue was amazed to see how a man could seem to disappear while you were looking directly at him. It was the coloration that helped some—buff moccasins, brown skin, dark hair blending into the rocky background. It was also the fact that by holding completely still Manolito made himself very hard to see among the trees.

Blue hoped that he was doing as well on his side of the trees. He worried about the light color of his hair giving him away, and so he did not look over the top of rocks but always around the side instead.

He wormed forward on his stomach the last twenty feet to the end of the ridge, and then he saw where the smoke was rising from several small fires.

His first impulse was to leap up and shout as loud as he could and then go running toward the camp down there where a green ribbon of grass extended a short distance from a spring in the rocks.

It was a camp of cavalrymen!

What held Blue in check for those first few seconds was something not easily understood. Afterward, he guessed it was because a sense of caution about everything he saw had been beaten into him by his experiences of the last few weeks.

He kept staring. The scene was real. They were soldiers. About fifteen or twenty, he estimated. All he had to do was walk down the hill and join them. He looked over to see how Manolito was taking it. Mano had been there a few moments before but now he was not in sight.

The soldiers had picked a very poor campsite. There was a spring issuing from the rocks, but there was scarcely any grass for the horses. It was still fairly early in the afternoon. Why hadn't they ridden on to a better campsite?

Something rasped on the stiff limbs of the oak brush below Blue. He nocked an arrow and waited. Manolito's dark head appeared. He crawled uphill to lie beside Blue.

"Why didn't you go down there?" Mano asked.

"I almost did, but the way they're hiding out down in the rocks like that—"

"It struck me, too," Manolito said. "I think they know where Cayatano's camp is. If they don't, they probably have scouts looking for it. Like Apaches, they know the best time to strike is at dawn, and that, I think, is what they have in mind."

"We don't want them to do that!"

Manolito stared at the soldiers. "I have a long memory for those who have done me wrong. I remember the rope around my neck and stones they put on my back. Who can forget such things? But still I did not give a great shout when I saw the soldiers."

"We don't want them to attack the camp!" All the little children, the women, even the men whom Blue had hated with all his heart only a few weeks before—and Cayatano himself, who was trying his best to keep his people at peace. . . . No, Blue thought, no!

"Perhaps they have been sent to rescue us," Manolito said. "If that is so, it is lucky for us that we saw them first."

"That's it! That's why they're here. Once they know we're all right, they won't bother Cayatano, so let's—"

"It is not that simple, *amigo*. They are soldiers, and they are commanded by some officer who has orders to kill Apaches. If we go to them, we will make it even easier for them to strike the camp, because then they will not have to worry about captives."

"You don't think we could talk them out of it?" Blue said. The soldiers were so close. . . . It was such an easy thing to go to them. Not to go into the camp was like turning your back on home. "We can make them understand about Cayatano."

"I have never had any success talking to officers of any army," Manolito said. "It is my opinion that most of them are selected on the basis of arrogance and great stupidity, and they always say, 'We have orders that must be carried out.' Only once in my life was I happy to see soldiers."

Blue had an inspiration. "Suppose one of us goes back to Beyota to tell Cayatano, while the other goes down to the soldiers. That way Cayatano can decide what to do."

Manolito shrugged. "It is the officer down there who will decide what to do. You go down and I will return to camp."

It was Blue's own idea but now it did not look very good. If only they knew what kind of officer led the detail, matters would be simpler.

"Do you wish to go down?" Manolito asked.

"No. Let's go warn Cayatano. He'll have plenty of time to scatter his people and get away—and then we can join the soldiers."

"That is my thought, too, *compadre*."

They backed away from the end of the ridge and started at a trot toward Cayatano's camp.

There were two people who thought their actions very strange.

On one of the higher ridges that overlooked the whole area, Kanseah and Itsee had been watching the soldier camp for some time. Looking for Soldado's scouts, they had seen a fine dust haze and thought it was being raised by a large group of Chiricahuas, and then the soldiers had come into sight.

They were the same ones Kanseah had met sometime before. Big Rifle was with them. If the soldiers had ridden up from the steep hills, Kanseah would have sent Itsee at once to warn the people at Beyota, while Kanseah would have stayed to watch the progress of the Pinda-lick-o-yi warriors. But the soldiers went into camp.

Now there was no great hurry, as Kanseah saw it.

Not long afterward, Itsee grunted and motioned with his head toward one of the lower ridges. Blue was slinking along that ridge, in and out of the rocks, stopping, hesitating. It took good eyes to see him. He was moving like an Apache.

Soon he would go far enough to see the soldiers, and then he would run to them. It was puzzling that, when he did get far enough to see the camp, instead of running down from the ridge, he disappeared behind the rocks and went no farther.

"He doesn't see them," Itsee said.

"Yes, he does."

They kept watching with great interest. Manolito— they knew he would not be very far away—crawled out of the oak brush and joined Blue behind the rock.

"Now they will go down together," Itsee said. "Then perhaps the soldiers will go away."

Kanseah and Itsee looked at each other in wonder as Blue and Manolito crept out of the rocks and went, not down to their own people, but back toward Beyota, trotting.

The two Apaches watched the soldier camp and

talked about the strangeness of the two White Eyes. Perhaps it was as Cayatano said: Not all of the White Eyes were the same. It was an unusual thing that Blue and Manolito had gone to warn the camp at Beyota.

Kanseah remembered how he had treated the two after capturing them. He was glad that he had respected his father's teachings enough not to kill them both, although they had been a great nuisance to him.

Lieutenant Bruton was having his difficulties. Three horses had gone lame that day, and that had held up the detail. Otherwise, according to Peeples, they would have been close enough to Beyota for the guide to go on in to determine whether Cayatano was camped there, and whether or not he actually had any captives.

It was a miserable camping place. Bruton had selected it intentionally in order to stay far enough away, he hoped, to prevent scaring Cayatano into flight. For two days the men had been forbidden to do any shooting, and now they were down to about the last scrapings of their rations.

They were grumbling and muttering among themselves. A few of them would have deserted, if they had not been so deep in Apache country. During the afternoon, when the detail was beginning to drag, Peeples had wanted to ride on by himself to the valley of Beyota, but Lieutenant Bruton had not been sure that he could find the spring without a guide.

Bruton gave orders to Sergeant McBride to post the guard, and then he went over to where Peeples was sitting on a rock. "You think they've spotted us, Tom?"

"Don't know how they could miss seeing us." The guide glanced up at the ridges above them.

"Do you think they'll understand that we're not planning to charge their camp?"

Peeples grunted. "Depends on if there even is a camp at Beyota, and whose it is. If you'd let me go on in—"

"We've been over that, Tom." It was still an Army detail. Bruton felt that he could not put the responsibility of recovering captives entirely in the hands of one civilian. He wanted to have the detail close enough to the camp to be effective, in case Peeples' efforts failed.

Because of the condition of the men and horses, he had not been able to go as far as he had hoped that day. He had planned to position the detail north of Beyota, but when he realized he could not make it, he had gambled on staying well away from the camp overnight.

"If they've seen us, and if they've run. . . ." Bruton shook his head. "We're in no shape to chase after them."

"Yep," Peeples said.

Dealing with Apaches who had captives was a rather touchy business, Bruton thought sourly. If he messed up the thing and the captives were killed, there would be fresh charges of Army incompetence. If he did not move firmly enough and the Indians got away with their prisoners, there would be a great uproar from the Apache-hating people of Arizona Territory.

Well, he would do the best he could. After he got the detail swung around on the north side of Beyota in the morning, Peeples could begin his negotiations. If, indeed, there were Apaches camped at Beyota.

And *if* they had captives. It could very well be that the

whole operation was directed against the wrong bunch of Apaches.

He wondered what had happened to Buck Cannon and Vaquero. Those two should have trusted him and told him the truth. That was the trouble: There wasn't a handful of citizens in the whole darn Territory who had any faith in the Army.

Lieutenant Bruton was fully aware of several good reasons why the citizens of Arizona Territory might be justified in holding the Army in low esteem. But on the other hand, he could think of a lot of reasons why the Army didn't think much of the citizens, either.

Buck and Vaquero were still very much in the game. From an oak brush thicket they peered down at Cayatano's camp. Sure enough, Manolito's horse was there in the herd with the rest of the animals.

But there was no sign of Blue and Manolito.

"Is it Cayatano's camp?" Buck asked.

"I don't know." Vaquero squinted at the wickiups. Women and children were the only ones in evidence. He had interpreted for John Cannon several times when the latter had talked to Cayatano, but each time there had been only Apache men with the chief.

He would recognize Cayatano at a glance, and there were two or three others that he could place. There was a huge, pockmarked man who limped, and Kanseah, and a young dark-faced boy who might have been of mixed blood. Yes, if he saw any of those around, he could be pretty sure that the camp was Cayatano's.

But none of them were down there.

Buck scratched his beard. "Well, we found an Apache camp, and now we don't know whose it is or what to do with it."

"The men are out hunting. When they return, it may be that I can tell more." In the meantime Vaquero had no intention of walking into the camp.

"Seems like there ought to be something we can do, instead of laying here like a couple of scared rabbits," Buck said. "How about catching somebody on his way in from hunting?"

"I would rather lie here like a scared rabbit and wait to see if someone I know returns."

"Not me," Buck said. "My patience is running sort of thin after all this time. If it isn't Cayatano's camp, let's find out."

"By capturing a returning hunter?"

"Yeah!"

It was the hard way, Vaquero thought, but if the camp was not Cayatano's, it was the only way to get information. He nodded. "Let us do our capturing some distance away from here."

They swung wide around the camp to where they had earlier seen tracks leading away from the little valley. Aware of the Apache habit of traveling ridges, they sought out a likely place to trap a man on his way back to the camp.

They found the ideal place. A game trail led along the side of the ridge above a dense thicket of oak brush. No hunter with game would care to force his way through the tough growth below. Moccasin tracks showed the route had been used by men going away from the camp; the chances were that they would return the same way.

The perfect spot was a mass of broken, jumbled rocks just above the trail.

It was indeed the perfect spot. As Buck and Vaquero reached it, preparing to set their trap, three Apaches rose up and covered them with rifles.

There they were, as if they had sprung from the very earth itself. Three lean, beady-eyed warriors, one directly in front of Buck and Vaquero, one on each side of them.

"Don't try it, *amigo*," Vaquero said. He put his arms out to the sides and let his bow drop to the ground.

Buck hesitated for an instant, and then he, too, obeyed the silent, deadly command of the rifles. "Cayatano's boys?"

"I'm afraid not."

One of the Apaches jerked the pistols and knives from their belts. "Soldado," he said proudly.

Buck wanted to groan. After weeks of living like wild animals, just when it seemed that they were getting somewhere, they had walked right into a trap.

The Apaches tied their hands behind them. Then they hustled the captives over the ridge and down the back side of it and into the oak brush, where they held a quick conference.

Minutes later, herding their captives ahead of them, the three Apaches set out at a fast pace. Buck threw a questioning look at Vaquero. They were not going toward the camp at Beyota, but were headed south.

"Later," Vaquero said. "Perhaps they understand a little English. Later I will tell you what they said."

That chance came when the Apaches stopped near the end of a ridge. Two of them went on ahead, while one squatted down to guard the captives.

"It is all a sad mistake," Vaquero said. "It *was* Cayatano's camp, but these three are of Soldado's band, and they have been after us for a long time, to get us away from Cayatano."

"What are you talking about, Vaq—"

"That is not my name, *amigo!* We are Blue and Manolito. Do you understand?"

Buck studied the Army pistol in the hands of the Apache guard. "I see. They think—sure!"

"Yes! One Mexican from the High Chaparral, and one man with blond hair. We are the ones, Blue and Manolito."

The three Apaches from Soldado's band had made a very simple, understandable mistake.

"Ransom?" Buck said.

"Oh, *si!* They will take us to Soldado now, and he will try to get a great ransom for us."

They had no way of knowing, and neither did their captors know, that Soldado had already sent a messenger to the High Chaparral in the name of Cayatano.

"How much will Big John have to pay?" Buck asked.

"Nothing. I am very well known to Soldado." Vaquero looked sidewise at Buck.

"You mean when old Soldado sees the mistake—"

"That is what I mean, *amigo.*" Vaquero drew his finger across his throat.

"You know something, Vaq—Manolito? We've got ourselves in a terrible mess. We've got to do something."

"I agree. What is the suggestion?"

Buck watched the pistol. The Apache was amusing himself by cocking it and pointing it at Buck's stomach. Since the gun was only a few feet away, the bore of the weapon appeared unusually large and ominous.

"What was the suggestion?" Vaquero asked.

"Well, right now I'd say let's not make any hasty moves."

"I agree to that, also."

About ten minutes later the two Apaches who had gone ahead returned and reported to the third one. The party backtracked for a short distance and then went over the ridge. It didn't take much figuring for Buck to know that they were avoiding something the scouts had seen.

"Soldiers," Vaquero muttered. "They saw some soldiers in a camp. The ugly one with the cartridge belt said that Big Rifle was there. Tom Peeples."

"It must be the same detail we saw at the river, huh?" They hadn't fooled Lieutenant Bruton with their story about stolen horses, Buck thought, or maybe Peeples had told him the truth. It was a little late now, but he wondered if it wouldn't have been a good idea, after all, to have asked help from Bruton.

The Apaches were in a tremendous hurry. They drove their captives at a pace that tested the very limits of their endurance. Going down the steep hills it was difficult to maintain balance with their hands tied behind their backs, but Buck and Vaquero did the best they could.

Sometimes they fell, rolling against bushes or rocks before they stopped. They found it best to get up as quickly as they could, since their captors were eager to aid them to their feet with savage kicks and jolting blows from rifle butts.

Dusk came and the Apaches kept pushing on at a relentless pace. It was not the soldiers they were afraid of, Buck was sure. Fear of pursuit from Cayatano's camp was the spur that was driving them.

Buck didn't know how far he was from the truth. Cayatano didn't even know that Buck and Vaquero had been close to his camp, let alone the fact that they had been captured by Soldado's scouts. No one was going to come after them. No one at all.

It did not help Buck's thoughts of escape when soon after dusk a fourth Apache caught up with them.

Vaquero listened to the slurry talk and told Buck, "This one read the tracks. There are two others somewhere behind us yet. They, too, will probably catch up soon."

"Only six to two," Buck panted. "That's pretty fair odds. Something will come up to give us a chance."

15 Returning Friends

BLUE AND MANOLITO came into camp at full tilt and ran straight to Cayatano's wickiup. The chief had just risen from a long nap, and so had Nonithian, though he would have said his nap was for the purpose of having important dreams.

The medicine man and several hunters who had returned a short time before trotted over to Cayatano's wickiup after seeing Manolito and Blue arrive in such haste.

Quite calmly the chief repeated what he had just learned from the two runners.

"Soldiers!" Nonithian cried. He pointed an accusing finger at Blue and Manolito. "I said they would bring soldiers on our trail!"

"Who warned us of the soldiers?" Cayatano asked quietly. "Who ran to tell us?"

Nonithian blinked. He had overlooked an impressive fact in favor of Blue and Manolito. "It is a trick!" he said. "The soldiers are not camped. They are riding to strike us as we stand here talking."

Some of the men grunted assent and gave Manolito and Blue dark glances. The women overheard Nonithian's loud talk and became excited. They called to their children and began to run about, gathering up their possessions.

Manolito addressed himself to Cayatano. "The soldiers are camped where I have said. They will not ride tonight."

"It is a trick!" Nonithian said. "I saw it in a dream."

For once Cayatano cut him off before he could begin his long expounding of a dream. "I will go myself to see the soldier chief."

"And they will kill you," Nonithian said.

"No!" Manolito said. "Bloody Head and I will go with Cayatano and see that no harm comes to him."

"They will kill Cayatano," the medicine man insisted. "Pinda-lick-o-yi soldiers can never be trusted."

Cayatano looked at Nacori and motioned toward the meadow downstream where young boys were guarding the ponies. Nacori trotted away to get the chief's horse.

Nonithian was still warning of dire things to come, when Cayatano rode away. Nacori, Manolito, and Blue trotted behind the chief's horse. They had gone about two miles when they met Itsee.

"Kanseah still watches the soldiers," Itsee reported. "They will be very angry when they know what has happened to their scouts."

"What has happened to their scouts?" Cayatano asked.

"They have been captured by three of Soldado's men. I saw them being taken away." Itsee pointed south.

"Did you know the scouts?" Cayatano asked.

Itsee shook his head. "I know Big Rifle, who lived with us. He is in the soldier camp. I did not know the scouts who were captured. They wore moccasins. One had pale hair. The other was tall and dark. Their hands were tied. Tahzi and Flat Nose and another I did not know were taking them away. Now the soldiers will be angry."

"I will tell them that it was no one of our clan who took their scouts," Cayatano said. "Then they will have no reason to be angry at us."

Itsee was doubtful. "Soldiers are mad at all Apaches all the time. I will not go into their camp." He thought a moment. "Perhaps they do not know about their scouts yet. It was only a short time ago."

"I will tell them," Cayatano said.

"Then I will not go into their camp."

Itsee accompanied them to where Blue had lain and watched the soldiers, but he would go no farther. Blue hailed the soldiers from the hill, identifying himself.

"It's a trap!" someone shouted in the camp, and there was a great leaping around to seek cover.

Not until Tom Peeples worked his way up the hill far enough to converse easily with Blue was Lieutenant Bruton satisfied about his identity. And then Cayatano stepped out of the rocks and talked to Peeples.

After that, it still took a great deal of shouting between the guide and Bruton before the lieutenant gave his permission for the group to come on down to the camp.

Peeples and Cayatano greeted each other cordially. With dignity that ignored the cavalrymen crouched behind rocks with their carbines ready, Cayatano walked up to the lieutenant and shook hands. Then he said in

English, "There is one more man on the hill, and that is all. He was afraid to come here."

"I regret that I cannot speak your language as well as you speak mine," Bruton said.

Cayatano stared for a long moment at the lieutenant. It was strange for a White Eyes soldier to say such a thing. Perhaps this leader of soldiers was another one like the Gray Fox, who believed that Apaches were men.

From that moment on, Bruton and the Chiricahua chief got along very well. The lieutenant studied Blue and Manolito. "You are returning the captives and want no ransom?"

"I am returning our friends," Cayatano said. "If they had stayed longer, they would have become true Apaches."

Manolito nodded. "It is a long story, but there is truth in what he says. Except that he was afraid we would run into Soldado's men, he would have released us anytime."

Blue heard one of the soldiers grumbling to a companion, "They look better fed than us. Maybe we're on the wrong side, Billy."

Peeples was eyeing Nacori sharply. He spoke in Apache to Cayatano. "Where'd this one come from? He looks—"

Manolito interrupted smoothly, also in Apache, "Yes, he looks like one of my cousins, far removed, who long ago lived with the Apaches and had three wives. Who knows, perhaps he is a cousin, but he was born an Apache and he *is* Apache, the son of Cayatano."

It was hard to say whether or not Peeples swallowed

the story whole, but at least he understood. "Ah, yes," he said, switching into English, "I remember him now from when I lived with Cayatano's clan."

While the others settled down to talk, Blue wandered around the camp. The soldiers were only partly relaxed; they were still keeping an eye on the hills above them, a long rifle shot away. They asked him questions that he found difficult to answer, for they were based on a lack of understanding of Apaches.

He was somewhat surprised to know how greatly his attitude toward Apaches had changed. It was easy now to understand some of the things Pa had talked about, but it was far from simple to put them in words to the soldiers.

Eventually he came down to statements that really didn't mean much but seemed to satisfy the questioners. "Oh, we got along all right." Or, "Yeah, it was sort of tough at first." And, "We learned how to shoot a bow pretty good."

Too much had happened to him and Manolito for it to be explained readily to strangers. He could do better, he thought, telling about it all to Pa and Victoria.

It was done. There was nothing left now but to go home. He heard Lieutenant Bruton telling Cayatano that the detail would start back to Camp Grant in the morning.

And then Cayatano said, "It was not my people who took your scouts and hurried south with them. Itsee saw them. They were Chiricahuas from Soldado's band."

"I don't understand. I had no scouts."

A slow, cold fear began to grow in Blue as Cayatano

described the scouts. He had heard Itsee tell about them, but now the description took on a different meaning. Buck and Vaquero? No, it couldn't be!

Blue went over to where the chief and Bruton were sitting. He knew by Manolito's expression that Mano, too, was shaken.

The lieutenant and Peeples looked at each other for a moment. The guide nodded gravely.

And then Bruton said, "That was Buck Cannon and Vaquero. They stayed with us in the big canyon a few days ago."

"You're sure?" Blue cried.

Peeples looked at him and nodded. "They'd been on your trail for weeks."

It was not over, Blue thought bitterly. It was just beginning.

Manolito rose and put his hand on Blue's shoulder. "We'll get on the trail and go as far as we can before dark."

"Itsee and Kanseah will go with you," Cayatano said.

Nacori rose. "And I will go."

For a moment Cayatano hesitated, and then he nodded, giving his approval to Nacori.

"I can give you some men," Lieutenant Bruton said.

Peeples shook his head. "Footwork. You haven't got a man in the whole detail who could keep in sight of these youngsters."

"We have enough as it is," Manolito said.

Peeples went back up the hill with them to where Itsee was waiting. The prospect of a chase and a fight brought a happy gleam to Itsee's eyes. He was ready to go as soon as the word was given.

He spat on a small steel mirror, polished it on his breechclout, and began to signal Kanseah on the high hill. The reply came back in a few brief flashes of light. "He will meet us," Itsee said.

Blue continued to stare at the high hill, remembering how it all had started from a single wink of sunlight from Kanseah's mirror only a short distance from the High Chaparral. It seemed like a long time ago.

Everything was turned around now. The same Apache who had captured him and Manolito was going with them to help rescue Buck and Vaquero.

Blue shook hands with Cayatano. He wished that he had time, and the words, to thank the old chief for many things. Cayatano studied his face and seemed to understand, and then the old Apache pointed toward the oak brush where Itsee and Nacori had already disappeared.

Blue and Manolito trotted away.

From the next ridge they caught their last look at Cayatano. Peeples was going back to the soldiers. Cayatano was walking on slowly to where he had left his pony.

Itsee and Nacori had already gone over the ridge, assuming that Manolito and Blue would follow their tracks as well as any Apache. They managed to do that, and they went at least a mile before they found their companions, who had been joined by Kanseah.

Itsee pointed out the tracks made by the three Chiricahuas and their captives. Kanseah's eyes gleamed with the prospect of a fight as he looked to the south across gray, jumbled hills.

Cayatano had told Blue that many years before members of Soldado's clan had intruded into a part of the land where the Wormwood clan was picking mescal. There had been a fight and two of Cayatano's people had been killed. One of them had been a medicine man, the father of Nonithian.

Though Itsee and Kanseah had not even been born at the time, they knew the story well. It was enough to make them hate Soldado's clan and all who banded with them. It seemed strange to Blue that Cayatano, whose dream was to stop the internal warring of Apaches, had not hesitated in sending two of his sons and Itsee into a certain fight with Soldado's men.

The answer was, perhaps, that Cayatano already had the hatred of Soldado. He had nothing to lose there, but all Apaches might suffer if Buck and Vaquero were killed.

Nacori said, "If we had some plan to get the two White Eyes from Soldado's scouts without killing any—"

"It will not be possible," Kanseah said flatly. "We must kill all the scouts."

Itsee was staring thoughtfully across the hills. "We know there are three, but there may be more who will join the others. They will set traps for us."

"No matter how many traps they set, we will kill them all," Kanseah said disdainfully.

"Two of them are Tahzi and Flat Nose," Itsee said. "They will not die easily. I know about them."

"Are you afraid?" Kanseah asked scornfully.

"No one is afraid," Nacori said. "Let Itsee say what he has to say."

"Let him speak, while the trail grows old, and the leaves fall, and the snows come," Kanseah growled. "Let us be afraid to fight, and stand here until the two White Eyes are roasted over the fire, and the birds are picking their bones. Let us stand here like women, talking, when—"

"Who is delaying us with more talk than Nonithian himself?" Manolito said. "Let Itsee speak."

Kanseah scowled but he held his peace.

Itsee's plan called for one man to stay on the trail. The other four would go on as fast as they could to get ahead of Soldado's men, with the idea of setting their own ambush. Once the general pattern of the flight was established beyond doubt, the tracker would swing around Soldado's scouts and join his companions.

It seemed clear that Soldado's men were headed for the Salt River, so why lose time by having everyone follow the tracks?

Nacori volunteered to stay on the trail. They would all meet sometime the next day at the Cave of Bones in the great canyon and plan their next move. Even though Soldado's men would be slowed down by their White Eyes captives, it would not be possible to overtake the party before they reached the canyon.

If he hadn't learned it before, Blue found out that day why horses were not a necessity in the Apache way of life. Before dusk, Kanseah led them a full twenty miles at a tireless trot. Night slowed them but they still kept going at a steady pace through a moonless dark.

It was mid-morning of the next day when they came down the last steep hill and reached the bottom of the great canyon near the Cave of Bones.

After he drank from the river, Blue wanted to lie down in the warm sun and sleep, but he went with Kanseah when the Apache insisted on casting about for tracks. A quarter mile downstream they found fresh tracks.

There were six men in the party now. Blue wasn't sure that he could have told that much by the tracks in the sand at the edge of the river, since the marks overlaid each other. Since they were all made by moccasins, he asked Kanseah how he could be positive that two of them were white men.

Kanseah pointed at one pair of moccasin tracks and made a V with two fingers to indicate how the feet had been toed out. "All Pinda-lick-o-yi walk that way."

Nacori was at the Cave of Bones when they returned. He had a pouch of jerky that one of Soldado's men had dropped. He shared it all around. They drank more water and then they started out again, Nacori still hanging to the trail, the other four following a dim, winding trail out of the canyon.

It was the same trail that most of Cayatano's people had used after they left the secret canyon and fled from Soldado's scouts. Farther up the canyon, Blue and Manolito saw steep, broken walls. It was somewhere in that area that Nacori had led them down during the eerie dawn while they sweated in terror.

Kanseah and Itsee went up the trail at a fast walk. Their legs seemed to be made of steel. They did not pant and they did not sweat. They were ruthless machines.

"I'll stay with them if it kills me," Blue said.

"It may kill us both, *amigo*," Manolito said.

Their next rendezvous with Nacori was to be at the Place of Many Kills. That was somewhere in the hills ahead, and that was all Blue and Manolito knew about the Place of Many Kills.

16 Brothers

AT DUSK Nacori came to where his companions waited in the junipers near a tiny spring at the head of a canyon. He came from the south, having followed the tracks several miles ahead of the rendezvous point.

"We are close upon them now." He described the place where Soldado's men were camped with the captives. It sounded very much like the place where Kanseah and the others presently were, dense junipers and other growth and probably a spring.

"Did you see them?" Blue asked.

"Two times. They have two captives."

"Did they see you?" Kanseah asked.

"It is possible. Two times one of them stayed behind and set an ambush, but I went around it and waited for him to join the others."

Kanseah was all for sneaking in for a dawn attack. "They think there's just one man following them. We can surprise them!"

"Not in that camp," Nacori said. "It is a bad place to attack. The captives would be killed."

Kanseah shrugged. "That is a chance that must be taken, no matter where we attack them."

"If the captives are killed, then all Apaches will be blamed," Nacori said. "Cayatano has said so many times." He turned to Itsee with an unspoken question.

Clown though he often was, Itsee had a shrewd head on him. "When we fled from our secret canyon because Soldado's scouts were close, the scouts had said that Soldado was not far away, with many men. Now I believe it was a lie. I think he was far away. If that is still true, tomorrow those with the captives will hurry fast and perhaps become a little careless.

"If in their hurry they leave the ridges and go down Yucca Wash, where there is a good trail, perhaps we can set a fine ambush there. We must surprise them quickly or there will be no captives to turn loose."

Even Kanseah had no objections as Itsee began to set out his plan. For the first time since the chase began, Blue fully realized that fighting and killing were near. It made him scared and nervous. He had never killed a man and had no desire to do so, but now the lives of Uncle Buck and Vaquero were in the balance.

He would have to be as quick with decision and as disrespectful of human life as Kanseah or any other Apache. He wondered if he could do it when the chips were down.

In addition to their bows and arrows, both Kanseah and Itsee had pistols. Though Cayatano had frowned upon it, Nacori had taken a rifle at the last moment before leaving Beyota. Manolito and Blue had only their bows and arrows.

"We lack skill with the bow," Manolito said to Itsee, "so you and Kanseah must give us your pistols."

"Perhaps tomorrow," Kanseah said.

"Now. We want to clean them."

Kanseah and Itsee hesitated, looking at each other. Though they were all on the same mission, Apache distrust for the white man was still strong.

Nacori stepped forward and gave his rifle to Manolito. "It is old and sometimes it does not fire, but you can use it."

Manolito nodded his thanks. It was indeed an old firearm, a Spanish flintlock that appeared not to have been cleaned in ten years. From his pouch Nacori produced a small metal powder bottle and some greasy balls.

As if shamed by the act, Kanseah said, "I have seen Nacori try to shoot that rifle." He shook his head, and then he gave Manolito his weapon. Like Nacori's, it was very dirty and had received little care to protect it against rust, but it was a modern pistol with fixed ammunition.

Itsee gave his pistol to Blue. "They have rifles, Soldado's scouts, but I can shoot arrows faster than they can fire their guns," he bragged.

Manolito and Blue busied themselves cleaning the weapons. They tore patches from their breechclouts and trimmed small sticks from a juniper tree for cleaning rods. They swabbed the bores of the pistols with water and cleaned the dust and grit from the cylinders. Apaches regarded weapons the same way they viewed horses—something to use, with no concern for upkeep.

After dark Kanseah built a tiny fire and threw on a rabbit he had killed that day. He had neither skinned nor gutted it. Blue knew it was not going to roast for very long. He wanted to cook his share of it on a stick but he knew better than to violate Apache custom by cutting or puncturing cooking meat.

Like the others, he ate his share half-raw.

Since Nacori was sure that their quarry was camped for the night, Itsee said they could sleep for a time before going on, but soon after daylight they must have their trap set.

Blue dozed fitfully. His mind kept going over his first few days as a captive, when all that he and Manolito could think of was different ways to kill Kanseah. And now Kanseah was sleeping peacefully a few feet away, while he and Manolito were now armed with loaded pistols.

He felt the rope scars on his neck. Manolito had joked about them, saying that people would see them and say that Blue and Mano were horsethieves who had been cut down when only half-hanged by a posse. That did not seem very funny to Blue.

But he guessed he could carry the scars without too much fretting. Maybe he could even look upon them with pride in time. Not many men had gone through Apache torture and lived to tell about it.

Considering what he had been through at the hands of the Apaches, he could not quite understand why he didn't hate all of them. He knew it would be almost impossible to explain his attitude to others who regarded all Indians as brutal, depraved people, not quite human.

They *were* brutal, of course, and their ways were different from the white man's customs and beliefs. Maybe that was where the understanding had to begin, with just the simple fact that Apaches were Indians. They could not be made into white men overnight, any more than a white man could be converted into an Apache in a short time.

Blue guessed it was too big a problem for him to wrestle with. He knew he had been trying to keep his mind off something else that was more immediate.

It was tomorrow that worried him. Suppose he didn't measure up when the time came? The way Itsee had things laid out, it would be wild, flaring action for only a few moments, and if one of them didn't do his part, one or even both of the captives could die.

Blue rolled uneasily on his bed of juniper needles. What if he failed and had to go back and try to explain it to Pa? His own childish stubbornness about a few simple chores around the High Chaparral had started the whole thing, Blue told himself. That seemed so long ago and so silly that he wondered why it had even happened.

He fell asleep and dreamed that he was pointing his pistol at a big Apache who was coming at him with a knife. No matter how hard he tried, he could not pull the trigger.

Nacori woke him by shaking his shoulder. "You were moaning in your sleep, Bloody Head."

Itsee roused not long afterward. "It is time to go."

An owl hooted just as they left the camp.

The three Apaches stopped dead in their tracks. Moments later the owl hooted again, and then it flew past, unseen in the blackness, its wings making a hushed noise.

Nacori, Kanseah, and Itsee stood silent, unmoving.

"What is it?" Manolito asked. "What's the matter?"

"The bad sign," Nacori said.

"Death," Kanseah said.

"When an owl calls in the dark near a camp, it is the sign of terrible things," Itsee explained. "We must go no farther or some of us will be—"

"It was not a camp," Manolito said. "We had left it, and so it was no longer a camp."

The Apaches were not impressed by this reasoning; they huddled together and said nothing.

"Owls must hoot somewhere," Manolito said. "It is their nature. Would you have them silent all the time?"

"It is a bad sign when they make their sounds near a camp before dawn," Kanseah argued.

"It was not a camp. We had left it. Even the owl realized his mistake and flew away," Manolito said. "Now if we stay here, perhaps the owl will return, so we must go swiftly and travel far."

The Apaches were shaken. They talked of dropping the mission and returning to the river. Manolito kept arguing persuasively about the habits of owls, and he said that he had dreamed of a quick and complete victory over Soldado's scouts. He said a mother coyote had talked to him as he slept, telling him that Itsee's plan was wise and good.

The account of his dream was almost as vivid as one of Nonithian's long tales.

At last he got the Apaches to go on, though they were

morose and worried about the hoot of the owl. After they started, however, they showed a great determination to put as much distance as possible between them and the camp. Under the pale starlight they moved at a pace that put a heavy strain on Blue and Manolito.

The general run of the country seemed vaguely familiar to Blue. They were going downhill, and the feel of the desert was out there in the dimness. He was sure they had gone far beyond the high hill where Kanseah and Itsee had tried to trick him into an escape effort.

Dawn was not far away when they trotted down a rocky hill and came into a wide wash where scrubby mesquite grew. Itsee stood for a few moments, peering around him, and then he led them directly to a sandy place where the mesquite bushes were small and thinly scattered.

Following Itsee's orders, they went to work quickly. First, they uprooted some of the smaller bushes. Then each man dug into the sand and rocks until he had created a depression large enough to conceal most of his body when lying prone.

Only Nacori, who was to put the final touches on the ambush, had no place of concealment. He helped Blue dig with his hands. At the head of each narrow trench they reset the mesquite bushes. Each man got into his trench and scraped all the sand he could reach over him. Nacori completed the operation, placing rocks carefully, sprinkling sand on the bodies of the ambush party.

Once settled into his hiding place, Blue had to dig two rocks from under his chest. Manolito was on his right and Kanseah was on his left. They were not buried under the sand, but they were covered sufficiently with it so that they blended into the barren wash.

Nacori's final work had to wait until full light. With a mesquite bush he carefully smoothed out all tracks and other signs around the ambush pits. Leaping from rock to rock in order to leave no tracks himself, he went a short distance from the site and viewed it critically, and then he carefully returned to make alterations or additions.

He did this several times before he was satisfied, and then, scrubbing out the single-file tracks they had made descending into the wash, he went up the hill the way they had come and took concealment among the rocks.

It seemed to Blue that they were starkly exposed. They were lying in an open space, with the trail only about fifteen feet away, with no cover close to it. Already he felt himself becoming hot and cramped as he peered almost at ground level through the thin screen of the mesquite bush near his head.

Nacori had sprinkled sand in his hair, and now it was beginning to make his scalp itch.

"Be still. No moving," Kanseah warned. "Do not make the bad things the owl said come true."

Kanseah and his miserable owl, Blue thought. He was thirsty and hungry. Only his right hand and his pistol were completely uncovered, below the level of the pit.

And now it was nothing but waiting, the very hardest part of the whole thing.

Blue's neck muscles began to cramp. He lowered his head slowly and rested it on his free hand. Before long the sun had burned all coolness from the air and was bearing down on the wash with scorching force. Blue remembered how cool it had been in the little green valley of Beyota.

Sweat dripped from his face onto his hand. He wondered if the pistol had become fouled with sand while Nacori was covering him up. If the barrel was choked with it, the weapon would blow up in his face when he fired it. Without uncovering his wrist and arm, he tried to work his hand enough to tilt the pistol to let any sand in the barrel run out. But the barrel was already slanting upward, and he could not tilt it down without disturbing his covering.

Sand had worked inside his breechclout and under the thin shirt Pinera had given him. He remembered how she had looked at Manolito with stony-faced resignation when they were leaving camp for the last time.

He tried to think of anything under the sun, except what he had to do before long. How long? Maybe they wouldn't even come this way.

Blue closed his eyes and waited. Time dragged on leaden feet and the sun grew hotter.

A tiny scraping in the sand caused him to open his eyes sometime later. Two scorpions were moving close to his buried arm, their stingers curled, their pale yellow bodies repulsive in the sunshine. It took all Blue's willpower to keep from moving.

The scorpions went over his fingertips, within inches of his face. Making small cascades of sand, they went up the edge of the pit and disappeared. Blue let his breath out in a long sigh.

Hours later Kanseah murmured, "They are on the trail!"

Blue raised his head slowly. They were at the head of the wash, coming fast. Uncle Buck, hatless in the hot sun, and Vaquero were in the lead.

There were six Apaches with them!

"Wait for Nacori, *amigo*," Manolito said calmly. "Remember, wait for him."

Blue cocked the pistol. He forgot to hold the trigger back and the weapon made a sharp click. It did not matter, as far away as the Apaches were, but it reminded Blue of all the things he might forget to do when Nacori called out from the hillside.

He watched them come down the trail. Buck and Vaquero were moving on heavy legs, weary, lurching at times. They were looking everywhere around them, those lean, brown Apaches. It seemed incredible to Blue that they would not spot the ambush.

They came on at a trot. Blue heard the swish of moccasins. He was holding his breath. He did not realize the fact until he was forced to let it out and fill his lungs.

Now they were very close. Vaquero grunted as he stumbled and almost fell. Uncle Buck passed. His face was heavily bearded, with a gray tinge to his whiskers.

And then Nacori shouted.

Blue heaved up on hands and knees, high enough to see above the mesquite bush. Four of them were bunched together. Two others were farther back on the trail. Nacori's yell had distracted them, held them for just a moment.

And now the men who had erupted from the pits caught them completely by surprise.

Manolito's pistol roared and Blue saw an Apache make a half-spin and go down. An arrow appeared as if by magic in the chest of another man. Blue knew that he was slow, but now he picked an Apache who was stringing an arrow. He fired and saw the man double over and fall facedown.

After that, everything was a wild, confused blur of action. Nacori's rifle boomed on the hillside. The slamming crash of Manolito's pistol went on and on. An Apache was coming in with a knife held low. Blue fired at him point-blank. Arrows sprang suddenly from the man's chest and throat. His momentum carried him close to the pits before he fell.

And then there was no one close who was still on his feet. Through a haze of choking black-powder smoke Blue saw a man dodging through the rocks. He fired at him until the pistol clicked twice on empty chambers.

An arrow skidded off a rock as the running Apache darted behind it. With incredible speed on the steep pitch, the man kept going, twisting his way through the rocks, never exposed for more than a moment or two.

Blue lowered his pistol slowly. It was over and he felt a stunned sense of relief. Of the five men on the ground, only one was moving. As Blue stared down at him, Kanseah drove an arrow into the man's heart.

Manolito was soon pounding Blue on the shoulder, grinning at him. Blue looked around wildly. "Uncle Buck! Uncle Buck!" he yelled.

"Well, blessed day in the morning!" a voice said, and

Buck Cannon rose from where he had dived behind a scrawny mesquite bush at the first hint of ambush. Vaquero had been right beside him. He struggled to his feet and stared at Blue and Manolito, as if he could not believe his eyes.

"Genuine Apaches, both of them," Buck said. "Untie my hands, somebody. I want to hug the whole ugly bunch!"

Manolito and Blue cut the captives' bonds.

"You all right, Blue boy?" Buck asked.

"Why, sure. How about you?"

"Never better!" Buck yelled. He held his swollen hands above his head. "Who are your friends?"

"Brothers," Manolito said.

Vaquero, too, was trying to get circulation back into his hands. "I know two of them, Kanseah there, and this one." He inclined his head toward Nacori, who had come down from the hill and who was now standing off to one side.

Itsee was searching the dead men, scattering their personal possessions carelessly, except for the cartridges he found in their pouches. Speaking in Apache, he said, "There are enough rifles for all of us."

"It will be good to have a rifle in my hands again," Vaquero said, and Itsee grinned at him, pleased to see that Vaquero could speak Apache.

Blue did not want to look at the dead men. Maybe he had helped kill two of them; he wasn't really sure, and he knew he would never brag about his part in the affair. He could not keep from watching, though, when Kanseah picked up a piece of cloth that Itsee had thrown aside, and put it over the face of the big Apache who had charged the pits with a knife.

Kanseah cast around in the wash until he found white stones to weight the corners of the covering on the man's face. "Tahzi," he said. "He was very brave. If we had not surprised them so well, he would have killed one of us."

"If the trap hadn't worked, there would have been more than one of us lying here," Manolito said. "Nacori froze them just long enough for us to get the jump."

"Just the same, it was bad," Kanseah said. "The owl warned that it would be bad."

"Yes, it was not all good," Itsee agreed. "One of them got away."

Kanseah looked up the hill where the man had escaped. "He dropped his rifle when he turned to run. It was Flat Nose who did that. If he had fought bravely, like Tahzi, I would have killed him."

"We will get him before the sun sets," Itsee said with a hard look.

He and Kanseah slung their bows on their backs. They took two of the rifles and left a few minutes later. As far as they were concerned, the mission would not be complete until Soldado's last scout was dead.

Blue watched them traveling swiftly through the rocks. That long-ago fight between the clans was not to be forgotten, and now there was fresh blood in the sand to keep the deadly enmity alive.

The women in Soldado's camp would cut their arms with knives and there would be a great wailing when it was known about the ambush, and the war among the

Apaches would go on and on.

But maybe someday Nacori could carry out the dream that Cayatano thought was possible. Cayatano had accomplished something already: There were four more white men who knew he was their friend.

Nacori said he would go with them until they were in sight of Sandy Lake. Though he took one of the rifles, he did not give up his flintlock. He offered it to Blue, but Blue shook his head.

"It is not like an arrow. It can be used again," Nacori said.

"What's he talking about?" Blue asked.

"An arrow that has killed a man must never be used again," Vaquero explained. "But a gun is different."

Blue still did not accept the rifle. A half mile down the trail, Nacori hid it in the rocks.

They camped that night beside a small stream. About noon the next day, from a high ridge, they saw the shine of Sandy Lake in the distance.

"Look at it. Just look at it!" Buck said.

When they turned to say good-bye and thanks to Nacori, he was gone.

"I think I know who he is now," Vaquero mused.

"Then you and I both have something to be quiet about, don't we?" Manolito said.

Vaquero nodded. "That is best, I think."

"I don't want to know any of your big, fat secrets," Buck said. "See that lake down there? I'm going down and wallow in it for about two hours before I even say hello to anybody."

Blue was the last to leave the ridge. He kept looking

north, trying to catch a last glimpse of Nacori in the bleak, gray landscape. But he could not see him. After a time he turned and followed the others on toward Sandy Lake.

Whitman CLASSICS

The Hound of the
  Baskervilles

Tales to Tremble By

More Tales to Tremble By

Seven Great Detective
  Stories

Black Beauty

Tales From Arabian Nights

Little Women

The Call of the Wild

Tom Sawyer

Robin Hood

The Wonderful Wizard
  of Oz

Robinson Crusoe

Wild Animals I Have
  Known

The War of the Worlds

Stand By for Adventure

Huckleberry Finn

Alice in Wonderland

Start your home library of
WHITMAN CLASSICS now.

REG. U.S. PAT. OFF.